TOPOGRAPHIES

TOPOGRAPHIES

JOHN SALLIS

Indiana University Press

BLOOMINGTON AND INDIANAPOLIS

This book is a publication of

Indiana University Press
601 North Morton Street
Bloomington, IN 47404-3797 USA

http://iupress.indiana.edu

Telephone orders	800-842-6796
Fax orders	812-855-7931
Orders by e-mail	iuporder@indiana.edu

The paper used in this publication meets the
minimum requirements of American National
Standard for Information Sciences—Permanence
of Paper for Printed Library Materials,
ANSI Z39.48-1984.

Manufactured in China

Library of Congress Cataloging-in-Publication Data

Sallis, John, date
  Topographies / John Sallis.
      p. cm. — (Studies in Continental thought)
    ISBN 0-253-21871-3 (pbk. : alk. paper) 1. Place (Philosophy)
  2. Sallis, John, date—Travel. I. Title. II. Series.
  B105.P53S35 2006
  910—dc22

                                                              2006001260

1 2 3 4 5 11 10 09 08 07 06

For Jim Risser
In Celebration of Friendship and Travel

Contents

Acknowledgments

I am grateful to David Krell, Nancy Fedrow, and Shane Ewegen for their generous help at various stages in the preparation of this book. Thanks also to my friend and editor Dee Mortensen, whose editorial expertise proved invaluable. Special thanks to Jerry for many of the photographs.

TOPOGRAPHIES

Foreword: Evocative Places

This is a book about certain places. Some are places I deliberately sought out; others I more or less chanced upon. In both cases they are places that proved to be evocative. What these places evoked were certain measures that in turn reflected back upon them; thereby each proved to be a site where some alterity or exorbitance or something archaic or elemental was disclosed.

This book is oriented primarily to these sites and to the disclosures they harbored. Yet the stories are also told of how I sought out these places or chanced upon them and of how I went about taking the measure of their evocative force. Hence, this discourse is, in part, narrative and in some respects even resembles a travel narrative told in first person.

Such a genre of discourse is by no means unprecedented. One could easily trace, along the margin of modern philosophical writing, a series of discourses that, deployed as travel narratives, are oriented to the disclosive openings that can be engaged through travel. Let it suffice to mention only a few instances, themselves incomparable: Goethe's *Italian Journey;* Hegel's *Report on a Walking Tour in the Alps,* as well as the letters that Hegel wrote during his extensive travels in the 1820s; Thoreau's *A Week on the Concord and Merrimack Rivers* and indeed, to some extent, nearly all his writings; and Heidegger's *Sojourns.*

This genre of discourse, though deployed in relation to travel, has nothing to do with tourism, either ancient or modern; neither is its orientation such as would simply exploit the figure of travel as a metaphor for the movement or development of philosophical thought. Rather, the travel to which such writing submits takes place as a discovery of evocative places, of places that, because they are evocative, give focus to the visit, in contrast to the accelerated distraction of tourism.

Focusing can take various forms, regardless of the scene brought into focus. It may be guided by a determinate expectation: one may come to a place with the intention of seeking confirmation for thoughts generated elsewhere and composed without any concrete experience of this place. Such would be the case if, in visiting Greece—sailing to Delos, for instance, or ascending the sacred way in Delphi—one's primary concern were to confirm, by what one could envision at such places, that the early Greek sense of truth was indeed as certain German poets and philosophers had taken it to be. Yet there are other ways to come to a place; one need not bring along, for confirmation, thoughts conceived elsewhere and elaborated without engagement with the place. Instead, one may set preconceptions in abeyance or, more precisely, let them recede into a horizon from which some may eventually be drawn out through engagement with the place. Focusing upon the place would, then, consist simply in becoming receptive to the scene offered. Evoked by the place, this focused receptivity would in turn open our senses decisively to the place's unique power of evocation. Or, more precisely, the place visited may evoke both focused receptivity and, yoked to it, a play of imagination. Through this double interplay, of receptivity and imagination and of both with the scene itself, a new thoughtfulness may emerge, a thinking that draws from the place rather than imposing on it, a thinking that draws from the place by letting itself be drawn to the place. Places would, then, be allowed to become protractive in the sense of engaging this double drawing.

I sought out various evocative places. Some I discovered in very foreign lands such as Japan and China: the site of a rock garden in Kyoto or of ancient bells in Hubei Province. In such places experiences are especially fragile, requiring a certain forgetting of who we are; and there is need for inscription to come to their aid if they are not to be lost. Other places I found in the mountains, especially in the Alps, where nature and culture have for so long cohabited that their disjointure, where it occurs, is all the more striking. I traveled also to ancient places, to places where the ruins of Western antiquity were to be seen. I visited Greece repeatedly, Athens of course and Delphi, but also the islands of the Aegean; for it was largely on the shores of the Aegean—on islands such as Samos and in coastal cities such as Miletus and Ephesus—that what came to be called philosophy began. Especially on the islands one can venture to reenact these beginnings as they were engaged with elemental nature, with the sea, for instance. In the western United States I visited the great canyons and began to understand that it is from such sites that we must learn the sense of the sublime and learn to pluralize that sense. I also chanced upon certain places that proved evocative, even some near my home, indeed at its very threshold. It was necessary then to install myself differently in these places and, to the extent that I could, to cast aside the veil of obviousness that obscures whatever is most familiar. But then I discovered, for instance, that from the scene of deer in the nearby forest something can be gathered about the very sense of home and of shelter.

While this book is thus about places, it is not about place in general, not about the concept of place. For place is not primarily conceptual; whenever one comes to frame a concept of place, one does so always on the basis of place experienced in its intuitive singularity. Thus the concept of place, place in general, place conceived in its generality, as a generality, is something secondary, derivative.

Yet this book is not even simply about place itself, about place as such in distinction from its concept. It is not about place as a pure intuitive singularity. It does not venture a new transcendental aesthetic. It does not even confront head-on the enigma that haunts place as such: that it is an intuitive singularity that is nonetheless not an intuitable singular thing. The enigma is that place as such is intuitive without being intuitable as such, that it is singular without being a determinate singular thing, an individual. This enigma is linked to another: that place cannot be accommodated to the traditional, metaphysical opposition between the intelligible and the sensible, that it is neither intelligible nor sensible nor something midway between intelligible and sensible. Drawing upon place itself in order to express this enigma, one could say that it falls outside the opposition between the intelligible and the sensible, outside in another place, in a place other than that of the opposition, in a place other than that which philosophy from Plato to Nietzsche has never ceased tracing, whether as a segmented line or as a story about true worlds and fables.

Though not directly confronting these enigmas, this book does not close them off. Indeed in some guise or other they permeate everything ventured here.

This book is, then, not about place but about places, singular places that are indeed intuitable, that offer their shape and their spectacle to our senses. It is a book about singular places that are evocative, about places that evoke both visions and words, about places that can become scenes of a gathering of sense.

These places are places of things, not in the sense of delimiting the boundaries of things, but rather in the sense that things are configured in these places, and the places themselves are shaped by things. What is ventured, then, is a writing imaginatively receptive to the evocative power of such places.

Each of the pieces in this book is geared to such a place, to a place where things and elements are configured in an exceptionally evocative—and thus disclosive—way. An exercise of vision is required, not just an observing of what is present, but a vision both anchored in the concrete scene and animated by the play of imagination. Only if this requirement is observed can one hope to gather what is wondrous in the sight of a waterfall or of a deer bounding into the forest, or in the sound of locusts invisibly performing their nocturnal polyphony, or in the happening of an outdoor festival celebrating, with fire, the summer solstice.

In and through evocative places there may be disclosures of manifold things, of animals in their proper setting, of humans in their capacity to engage life and nature beyond the bounds of the everyday. But, still more decisively, such places offer an opening upon the elements, not in the modern, chemical sense, but in a sense closer to that operative in the ancients' designation of fire, air, water, and earth (or rather, of what we translate by these words, by no means the same) as elements. The pertinent sense is also close to that which is operative when we say, for instance, that something or someone is exposed to the elements, that is, to wind, rain, snow, etc.

My travels brought me within sight of a glacier and allowed me to envisage the concurrence of elements in such a place. Witnessing a thunderstorm as it passed through a narrow valley provided another occasion for gathering a sense of the elemental; for the thunderstorm was nothing but a confluence of rain, wind, hail, thunder, and lightning. Also I repeatedly climbed high into the mountains, where everything recedes, falls away, except the bare, rocky earth and the brilliant dome of the sky. Even time receded, the time of those pursuing the everyday far below in the village; it gave way to a time more enduring than fleeting, a lithic time.

Each of the pieces in this book belongs to a time. The sequence is not insignificant, for there are connections between some of the pieces. Because the sequence is consequential and also because certain pieces extend toward other books composed during this time (most notably, *Force of Imagination*), I have given a date for each piece and ordered them according to these dates. Yet, except as marking the temporal sequence and exchange, the calendrical dates are relatively insignificant. What counts much more decisively are the times of year, the seasons, and even in many cases the time of day. Some elements belong to certain seasons, and some sights are to be seen in their elemental character only at certain times of day or perhaps only at night. Yet what counts is not only the time in which these scenes are set but also, as in the high mountains, the time that such places can disclose.

Focused receptivity to a place is also a receptivity to words, to words that come and that exercise in turn a kind of attraction on those held in abeyance, drawing these words out from the horizon. In the double interplay of receptivity, imagination, and the place on which they are focused, what emerges is blended from vision and words. Because of the intrinsic instability of this blend, there is need for it to be steadied somewhat by writing, secured in topographies.

Yet also there is need to refer these topographies back to the scenes to which they are linked. For this reason a number of images, mostly photographs, have been included, though there are of course some scenes that are so fleeting or fragile or mobile or segmented that they do not readily submit to being imaged.

Such reference as is thus provided to the visible spectacle is needed because the sensible image is such as to exceed the word, as the redness of a sunset exceeds what can be said in the word *red* or in a discourse deployed around this word. There is also excess in the other direction: the word exceeds the image in that the word posits a signification to which nothing seen or heard can measure up. One sees this animal or that animal there in a particular place; but one does not see animal as such. It is because of this double excess in the relation between image and word that their interplay has remained decisive in the history of philosophy from Plato to Nietzsche and remains, still today, an enigma with which thinking must engage. Topographies provide one way of carrying out such engagement.

On my travels I was often accompanied by family or friends, and this fact is indicated in the individual pieces by the plural form of the first-person pronoun. There is no estimating the enormous gift of dialogue I received from those traveling with me, and my gratitude to them is unbounded. This gift is in no way diminished by the experience that responding to these evocative places and writing about them is, beyond a certain limit, a solitary affair, even perhaps a discovery of a certain solitude.

Boalsburg
9 January 2005

1

Translations

Wuhan

Hubei Province

2 April 1988

Travel is exorbitant. It is transport beyond the circle of everyday familiarity, passage from the domestic toward the foreign. Even a limited excursion within one's homeland heightens the possibility of encountering
something unexpected, strange, uncanny. Travel to the border where
domestic and foreign intermingle has a more profound effect. But the
effect of travel beyond to another land is still more profound: then, like a
text rendered into another language, one is translated into a foreign context, carried over into it, transposed across the differential field separating domestic from foreign. Yet translation is not transformation, not an
exchange of identities. Traveling in a foreign land, one does not lose one's
foreignness; rather it is precisely then that one most experiences it. As
the translation of a text retains—except in the rarest instances—ineradi-
cable traces of its foreign origin, so is it also—to a higher degree—with
the traveler: even if one·arrives in the foreign land with some command
of the language and some knowledge of the land's history and culture,
one's foreignness will not go undetected, nor will one fail to experience
the foreignness of the land. To those native to the land, and to oneself as
well, it will be apparent that a translation has taken place, a translation
into the foreign land.

Translation into the foreign frames in deed the inaugural discussion of this differentiation, the discussion in which the very sense of one's own is first determined in distinction from what is other or foreign. Plato's *Republic*—in translation—opens with Socrates recalling an excursion: "I went down yesterday to Piraeus with Glaucon, son of Ariston, to pray to the goddess; and, at the same time, I wanted to observe how they would put on the festival, since they were now holding it for the first time. Now, in my opinion, the procession of the native inhabitants was fine; but the one the Thracians conducted was no less fitting a show." This place, Piraeus, was the site of the entire discussion reported by Socrates in the *Republic*. This discussion, which must have continued far into the night, concerned the *polis*. It sought to discover how the best *polis* ought to be constituted, to determine what would be proper to such a *polis*.

Piraeus was—and remains today—the port of Athens. It is located about six miles from the city and in antiquity was connected to the city by the long walls. As the port, it was the place where Athenians most readily came in contact with foreigners, the border area where domestic and foreign intermingled. Indeed the goddess Bendis, whose festival Socrates had come to observe, was a foreign goddess, recently imported from Thrace. Her festival, the Bendideia, was being held for the first time. At the festival there were processions both by Athenians and by Thracians; and the procession of the foreigners was no less fine, in Socrates' opinion, than that of the native Athenians.

That the discussion takes place in this setting is quite remarkable. The determination of what is proper to the *polis* is carried out at the place where Athens itself borders on the foreign. The discovery of what belongs to the ownmost nature of the *polis* is ventured in a setting where Athenians mingle with foreigners at a festival honoring a goddess more foreign than Athenian. In this setting Socrates, though singularly bound to Athens, begins nonetheless to undergo translation into the foreign. This setting thus suggests in deed that delimiting one's own requires that the foreign be brought to bear upon it and that, for the sake of such delimitation, one must venture into the foreign, must undergo translation into it.

This setting proves even more remarkable in view of what the *Republic* ventures at the center of its interrogation of the *polis*. Though treated ironically as a digression, the central Books of the dialogue venture the beginning of philosophy; more precisely, the discussion between Socrates and Glaucon, with whom he has come down to Piraeus, ventures both to say how philosophy begins and to enact this beginning through the very saying. Carried out in Piraeus, this beginning both in word and in deed is thus situated in the passage toward the foreign. And yet, in this beginning, what is one's own would not simply have been abandoned. Piraeus was connected to Athens by the long walls, so that by remaining between these walls one could go down to Piraeus without really having ever left Athens. The situation is not entirely unlike that of the prisoner who, as he ascends into the openness and light above, remains nonetheless bound to images; even as he emerges into the dazzling light, he remains bound to the condition of the cave, even as also he transforms it. Thus, in its beginning philosophy is situated within the passage to the foreign; it is engaged in the transition between what is one's own and what is other. Everything depends on whether philosophy remains in this transition, on whether it endures translation and persists in being translated; or whether it passes through the foreign only in order to take distance and thus to arrive at what is ownmost, at what—in a sense that is no longer primarily political—is most proper, most itself, indeed fully, self-identically itself. Everything depends on whether philosophy, beginning in the passage to the foreign, returns finally to itself or whether it remains in the transition, enduring being translated, persisting in translation even as it returns to its own.

Travel disturbs—even if only temporarily—the propriety of self, the proximity to self. In venturing to the border and beyond, the traveler undergoes translation into the foreign.

But what is the foreign? It is nothing as such; that is, there is no foreign as such; that is, there is no such thing as *the* foreign. For being foreign is intrinsically bound to the singularity of place. What is foreign in one place may well not be foreign in another. It is never simply a matter of foreignness in general, which would then be instantiated in particular foreign persons, things, or lands. Rather, in the determination of something as foreign there is always the third factor, place.

Both the place of origin and the place of appearance figure in the determination of someone or something as foreign. In particular, foreignness is determined by difference between place of origin and place of appearance: a person who is not native to a place, one who has ventured beyond the homeland, appears foreign to those who are native to this place. Much the same may be said of artifacts, practices, and cultural forms in general as realized, for instance, in institutions and in the arts: when transported beyond the place where they originated or otherwise belong, they appear foreign. Clearly the extent of the topical difference constitutive of foreignness is quite variable. In traditional societies, especially where such geographical features as mountains have an isolating effect, someone from the next valley, speaking a slightly different dialect, may be taken as foreign. Elsewhere people living thousands of miles apart appear to each other as belonging to the same homeland. The arts seem least prone to become foreign beyond the boundaries of their place of origin, all the more so when, as with music, they depend less—or even not at all—on language.

The place of origin, the place to which someone or something intrinsically belongs, is not a mere location but rather is the homeland. As such it is determined not only politically but also by certain homogeneities such as that of language. To appear foreign is to appear at variance with these homogeneities. The foreigner has prototypically been taken to be the one who does not speak the native language or who does not speak it natively—as, with the ancients, barbarians were those who did not speak Greek.

And yet, nothing is more decisive than that humans are not inescapably bound to their place of origin. Though usually native to one place or another, they are not bound to any place. In this regard the exception, nomadism—both in its traditional tribal guise and in its contemporary global form—is indicative of a decisive human possibility. To the metaphorics of human rootedness, it is imperative to oppose the effectiveness of human mobility. One can effectively leave behind the place where one happened to be born, even if, for a time at least, one will bear traces of that place in one's voice and gestures. Though there may be limits, depending on age and other factors such as education, one can become native to another place, not only living there (as a foreigner in exile) but integrating oneself more or less into the language and culture of that place, taking it over as one's homeland. It is indeed the assimilated immigrant, much more than the traveler, who comes to be translated into the foreign land to virtually the same degree that a good translation of a text renders that text in the other language.

The effects of immigration erode all efforts to establish—for a particular homeland—a rigorous determination of foreignness. One who appears in a certain respect foreign (for instance, an East Asian in a European setting) may prove to speak the native language perfectly and to be thoroughly integrated into the setting—that is, may prove not to be a foreigner. This phenomenon is compounded to the point of mutation in the Western Hemisphere, where almost the entire population derives from immigration.

Because such mobility is always to some degree possible, no one is absolutely foreign to any homeland. The alterity of the foreigner is always compromised by this possibility.

A person appears foreign to a place by way of certain signs that make manifest a divergence from the homogeneities distinctive of the place. Proverbially the foreigner is one who speaks differently, acts differently, and in many cases also looks different. By apprehending these differences, one identifies the foreigner.

And yet, such experience of the foreigner is limited, is one-sided. As long as the foreignness is apprehended in this way only, it is measured only by its deviation from what is one's own. The same one-sidedness will prevail, on the other side, when, transported to a foreign land, one is apprehended as a foreigner. What can supplement such experience and open onto a more comprehensive understanding is the experience of one's own foreignness in a foreign land. In this experience of one's being translated into the foreign land, there will be a double disparity. To another, to a person at home in the foreign land, one will appear foreign;

what is needed for understanding is that one recognize and interpret this appearing-other, engaging in dialogue to the extent possible. But, in turn, much of what one encounters in a foreign land will appear foreign; yet released to a much greater extent from one's own, the foreignness encountered in a foreign land can be interpreted in a way that is less one-sided, in a way that brings out its positive content rather than its deviation from domestic norms. Only through travel to foreign lands can one begin to experience foreignness in its integrity, to interpret it not merely as other but in such a way as to bring to light what constitutes it in its otherness.

The experience of one's own foreignness in a foreign land can claim no certain measures given in advance. The experience can easily be destabilized; then one either loses oneself in what is foreign or only asserts one's own against it and thus loses it. The experience is fragile, and for this reason words, even writing, need to be called on to secure to some degree what the experience can disclose. Such writing would have to be attuned to the foreign place in which the experience becomes possible. Its inscription would occur as topography.

It was my first trip outside the West. The flight seemed interminable: to the West Coast, then to Tokyo, finally to Beijing. I was met by a young Chinese couple whose friendliness showed far beyond their ability to express it in my language. Housed at Peking University, I took advantage of a free day to venture outside the walls of the university and to take an extended walk through the local neighborhood. Here for the first time I got a sense of my foreignness in this very foreign place: as I wandered among the vegetable stands, the Chinese—everyone else there was Chinese—stared at me, curiosity inscribed across their faces.

The next day we were assembled at the airport and flown to Wuhan. As we were driven from the Wuhan airport into the city, the scene was conspicuously other than what I had seen in Beijing: everything looked dirty and dilapidated, most of the buildings looked like hovels, and, above all, there were everywhere many, too many people. Later, as we were taken around the city to see the local monuments, I was most fascinated by the ordinary people alongside the street. They were cutting hair, repairing shoes, cleaning fish, cooking—all right out in the open next to the street, right where the sidewalk would have been, though most places there was only dirt.

There were eight of us together on the flight to Wuhan and a couple others who joined us later in Wuhan. I was the only American, indeed the only native English speaker. All the others were German. We had all come to China for an event that had virtually nothing to do with China or with Chinese thought. The bland title of the conference, "Theories of Man in German Philosophy," allowed the participants to speak on most any topic they pleased as long as it was treated within the context of German philosophy. Had it not been for the Chinese participants, it would have been a strange affair indeed, a group of Germans plus one American coming to China to discuss German philosophy! What was perhaps most interesting in the conference was the translational situation in which the various lectures were held. When I presented my lecture, which I had had to cut drastically to accommodate the translational situation, a young Chinese philosopher named Jin Xiping served as my interpreter. He had studied for three years in Tübingen and had reasonably fluent German but no English. A Chinese translation of my lecture ("Mortality and Imagination") had been prepared in advance, and, as I read my English text, I paused after each paragraph to allow Jin Xiping to read the corresponding Chinese. The most serious difficulties and the greatest uncertainty arose when it came to the discussion. When a question was posed by a Chinese participant, Jin Xiping improvised a German translation, which I had then to relate to my English text; my response had to be given in German to Jin Xiping, who then translated it into Chinese. The noncommunication, the noncorrespondence between question and answer, which I of course could not entirely gauge except through the testimony of Chinese with whom I could communicate, must assuredly have set me and my text apart as quite foreign. At the same time, the translational situation itself—even though I could not gauge it specifically—conveyed to me a profound—and strange—sense of my foreignness in this very foreign land. This foreignness was further accentuated by the contrast between this situation and that of my communication with the Germans, which now seemed hardly foreign at all.

When we were not occupied with the conference, we were escorted around Wuhan to various sights. There were three that proved quite astonishing and that served to enhance the experience of foreignness in this—for us—very foreign city to which we had been translated. One was the Kweiyuan Buddhist temple. When we arrived, we found that the area adjacent to the temple was filled with smoke, which had a strange smell that I could not identify. As we hesitated, not quite knowing whether to enter, a round of small firecrackers went off; we were told a little later that the firecrackers were set off in commemoration of a monk who had died the previous day. Closer inspection of the area outside the temple revealed that there were several large kettles in which people were putting what looked like pieces of paper, which they then set on fire—hence all the smoke. Finally we entered the temple and to our astonishment beheld five hundred Buddhas, every one of them with a different expression and gesture. The entire scene was utterly remote from anything that in the West would be affiliated with religion—indeed so much so that comparison with Western forms tended to fall away, and it became possible to enter more freely into what was there, present to sense, even as it remained utterly foreign.

Afterward we were taken to the Hubei Provincial Museum to see a set of sixty-five bronze bells that had been discovered in tomb excavations in Hubei Province in 1978. They are called collectively a *bianzhong*. Though buried since 433 B.C., they had been recovered almost entirely intact. When we heard them sounding (in a recording played for us), it was as though we were hearing the sound of antiquity, but of an antiquity other than our own, a foreign antiquity. Years later Tan Dun would compose a symphony around the sound of this *bianzhong* to commemorate the reunification of Hong Kong with China. His *Symphony 1997* combines the sound of the *bianzhong* with that of a children's choir, of a cello solo (written for Yo-Yo Ma), and of a modern orchestra. Beginning with a song of peace, this vast work traverses the entire creation from heaven, with its dragon dance and jubilation, to earth and the other elements, water, fire, and metal, to mankind, its lullaby, and again, in conclusion, a song of peace. There are few musical works that succeed so brilliantly in setting Chinese tonalities together, seamlessly, with the sound of the modern European orchestra without reducing the difference between them.

Yet the sense of the foreign conveyed by the temple and by the ancient bells, however remarkable it was in both instances, could not compare with what was evoked when we attended a performance by the Peking Opera. We arrived at the opera house early and so for a few minutes remained standing in an open space outside. It was almost dark, and as we—all Westerners—were talking among ourselves, I began to experience an uneasy feeling. Soon I realized that our small group had been completely encircled by Chinese. Their presence seemed almost threatening until I turned and looked directly at them. Then I could see in their stares and on their faces the utter curiosity that had led them to come so close to us. This experience of appearing foreign proved to be a fitting preview of what awaited us inside.

As we entered the hall, I noticed that the orchestra was situated on an upper balcony to the right, some distance from the stage. This placement betrayed that the relation between the orchestra and the voices would be quite different from the integration that Western opera achieves by placing the orchestra in a pit right in front of the stage. Before the opera proper began, the percussionists began playing, producing very strange sounds with instruments that sounded remotely like cymbals, various drums, and wood blocks. As long as one continued to hear this percussive prelude with Western ears, it sounded like loud banging on instruments that were less than refined. During the opera itself the percussion—set apart from the stage—often commenced sounding again, marking off (as far as I could tell) the various segments of the performance. There were also some string and wind instruments, which usually accompanied singing. Because of the orchestra's location high above the audience, it was impossible to get a full view. But there appeared to be five musicians, and they appeared to use no scores, though their playing seemed quite precise. It was also difficult to discern much about the instruments. The string and wind instruments appeared to be simpler than their contemporary Western counterparts, perhaps closer to those of Renaissance music in the West; indeed one wind instrument seemed at first to sound a bit

Faces of Peking Opera

like a krummhorn. Yet the combined effect of these instruments (including the very strange percussion) was so other that before long I was no longer even tempted to make comparisons with the sound of modern Western instruments. Instead, I began to be able to listen to them in their own right; it was not that their foreignness disappeared but rather that I became more adept at entering into these foreign sounds.

But foreign they remained. Since the arts are in general less prone to become foreign, since music in particular seems most resistant to appearing foreign, the foreignness of these musical sounds was all the more striking.

The translated title of the opera was *Journey under Arrest.* The story, set in the Ming dynasty, is quite simple. The prostitute Su San has been falsely accused of murder and thrown into prison. In order for her case to be reviewed, she must be transferred to another place. She is accompanied by Chong Gongdao, a subordinate of the local prison official. On the journey Su San tells Chong her tragic story, and he offers her consolation.

As soon as the opera began, I was struck by the beauty of the spectacle. The costumes were extremely elaborate and colorful, with long feathers and other ornamentation quite beyond—and quite other than—anything one would see in Western opera. The faces of the performers were elaborately made-up and in some cases beautifully painted, so that, together with the ornate costumes, the total effect was one of lovely extravagance.

The performance itself included a great deal of pantomime, dancing, and sheer acrobatics, though the principal characters maintained a dignified and elegant poise throughout the opera. To our Western ears the singing sounded very strange. Yet its strangeness was not just a result of its being sung in Chinese. In this case the foreignness went much further than in those instances in which a native English speaker, for example, hears an operatic performance in Italian, German, or even an entirely unfamiliar language such as Czech or Hungarian; for in these instances the singing as such remains Western, however foreign the language. But in the Peking Opera's performance, even recitative employed the voice in a way unfamiliar to Western ears: the pitch swung up and down, the voice rising and falling in a way that almost evoked the image of flight; though the tonal character of the Chinese language may suggest such a use of the voice, what one hears in opera far exceeds in this respect what one hears in ordinary spoken Chinese. The singing proper sounded still stranger, and its strangeness did not dissipate as the performance continued and it became easier to leave comparisons with Western singing aside. The pitch seemed abnormally high, and it had almost the quality of falsetto. It seemed that the voice came directly from the middle of the mouth rather than originating from deeper in the body and resonating in the throat.

Before I attended the performance with its unusual, predominantly percussive instruments, its acrobats, and its elaborately made-up and costumed characters singing in their seemingly falsetto, upward- and downward-swinging voices, I could not have imagined such a performance as I saw and heard that night in Wuhan. Its unimaginable quality is perhaps the best index of just how foreign—despite all my efforts to the contrary—it remained.

And yet, though foreign, what I had experienced remained with me, as I suspect it did also with those who shared the experience with me. What was most remarkable, however, was that it remained not just as an isolated experience retained in memory once I returned to the West.

Rather, the translation into the foreign that I had undergone in Wuhan gradually seeped into experiences that otherwise seemed bound entirely by my nativity. Coming back from the foreign to my own would prove to alter everything, if ever so slightly, not in such a way as simply to distance me from it, but in such a way as to make possible a certain understanding that would otherwise have remained out of reach.

It is not surprising, then, that Plato—also a traveler to foreign lands—concluded the *Republic* as he did. For the story in which Er, having come back to life, is made to tell about what he saw in the other world after death ends with a mystery and a hope. The mystery lies—as he attests—in his not knowing how he came back into his body. The hope, then expressed by Socrates, is for a good crossing, so that we shall be friends to ourselves and to the gods. Though discontinuous, everything depends on the crossing from the absolute foreignness of death, its utter alterity, to the life that is one's own. Nothing counts more than bringing the foreign back to one's own—

Unless it is repetition, repetition of this movement between one's own and the foreign. One could imagine engaging in such repetition, moving between one's own and the foreign, going down to Piraeus—or still farther—and returning to Athens. One could imagine doing so so constantly as to live primarily in and from the transition. At any rate this is what was both imagined and thought by a great American philosopher. In Emerson's own words, from his essay on Plato: "Our strength is transitional, alternating; or, shall I say, a thread of two strands. The sea-shore, sea seen from shore, shore seen from sea . . . ; and our enlarged powers at the approach and at the departure of a friend; the experience of poetic creativeness, which is not found in staying at home, nor yet in traveling, but in transitions from one to the other, which must therefore be adroitly managed to present as much transitional surface as possible; this command of two elements must explain the power and the charm of Plato."

2
Elements

Chantemerle, near Briançon
Hautes Alpes
15 August 1988

Nature resists categories derived from human fabrications. Whereas it can as a rule be shown that an artifact results from an imposition of form on a material, so that such concepts as form and matter are fully appropriate to such products, no such ready demonstration can be offered in the case of things of nature. Such concepts may of course be applied to natural things (and such application occurred already among the ancients); but, barring such a demonstration, the imposition runs the risk of doing violence to natural things. It is likewise with other concepts intimately linked to the techno-political structures of the human world, with concepts such as that of the foreign. Especially with things of nature that tend toward the elemental, the resistance to such concepts comes to border on complete exclusion. While a glacier-covered mountain may have prescribed how a certain political border is laid out, there will be little or nothing about the appearance of the mountain as such that would warrant applying to it the concept of foreignness. It bears no sign of foreignness comparable to that of a foreign-made artifact or a foreign practice. A glacier-covered mountain beyond the border of one's homeland will not appear significantly different from one on this side of the border. To be sure, mountains in widely separated locations may look different; but the difference derives not from the structures of the human world in these locations, but rather from geological factors, that is, from factors having to do with the earth.

Though it was late summer, there was still a good deal of snow on the mountain. As I looked up and out across a lower slope, now almost entirely green from the scrubby vegetation and scattered pines, I could discern the pattern on the mountain beyond. At various places rocky ledges or peaks provided shelter from the sunlight and allowed patches of snow to remain intact despite the summer heat. Nestled in the shadows, they appeared almost as white as newly fallen snow, though no doubt closer observation would have shown that rocks, dust, and other bits of earth had accumulated on them during late spring and summer, compromising the purity of their color. Perhaps these patches would be able to hold out into the fall, but my guess was that most would have disappeared entirely by the time the first snow of the coming winter arrived.

But with the glacier it was quite otherwise. Set in a huge concavity between the three highest peaks of the mountain, it was gigantic, and there were only a few places where ridges of rock protruded through its surface. Unlike the isolated patches, it was almost completely exposed to the sunlight; what allowed it to persist was not the shadow and shelter of mountain peaks but its own extent and density. Even from the distance from which I saw it, its surface appeared quite different from that of the patches of remaining snow; clearly it was not really snow but ice packed hard and dense by the enormous load of snow and ice that built up on it each winter. It had the look of something eternal, not in the abstract sense of an unlimited and undifferentiated present, but in the sense of something forever renewed in the cycle of the seasons. The mountain too had a certain look of eternity about it, but its eternity was one of absolute stability, an utter selfsameness akin to that of the earth itself. Both appearances bore a look of eternity belonging to nature rather than set apart from the expanse of natural things and elements. They were looks open to sense rather than closed off beyond it.

Most of the glacier surface was exposed to the sunlight, and especially along its edges it glistened brilliantly. Elsewhere, nearer the center, it was

Glacier near Chantemerle

not white at all but much darker, its color quite distinct from that of the snow. Curiously, its color appeared akin to that of the bare stone, which was exposed on the peaks as well as farther down the mountain; yet clearly the colors were not exactly the same. Though it would not be incorrect to say that the central surface area was light gray in color, it is perhaps more to the point to say that its color displayed a peculiar harmony, a resonance, with that of the mountain—letting these explicitly auditory metaphors say what they can about the visibility of things.

Yet what was most remarkable was the way in which the glacier caught the brilliant sunlight. Around its white extremity it reflected the sunlight, yet not at all as a mirror reflects something but rather in the sense of reproducing or translating the pure sunlight into the manifest whiteness of the glacier's extremity. Such translation is always necessary if light, by which all things are visible, is itself to become visible. Yet even more astonishing was the way in which the central area of the glacier's surface caught and translated the sunlight. Rather than rendering pure sunlight as pure white, this surface area translated the purity and transparency of the light into an opaque expanse akin to the mountain itself in color. It reflected the pure transparency of the light in an opaqueness akin to that of stone; it imaged light in earth.

With its glacier, the mountain offered a manifest gathering of the elements: light, gift of the fire of heaven, was reflected in ice and snow, themselves made visible by the very light they rendered visible in the reflection; in turn, the reflection was rendered opaque in the central area of the glacier's surface, was discolored, as it were, so as to reflect also the mountain stone, the earth itself as it towers up into the rarified air that the ancients called aither. In such spectacles nature sets before our imaginative vision a concurrence of these elements, of fire and light, water and ice, stone and earth, air and aither. At such sites nature displays a concurrence in which, gathered in their very opposition, each is shown forth.

3

Winter Stories

Radnor Lake
Tennessee
25 December 1990

The lake and its heavily wooded surroundings have become a sanctuary for wildlife and a natural haven for anyone seeking respite from what passes for life in modern, urban society. Yet Radnor Lake did not come about by nature, not at least in the beginning. Nearly a century ago it was formed by damming up Otter Creek so that the rainwater runoff from the surrounding hills would accumulate rather than being carried away. In fact the lake was formed not with a view to nature and to the thriving of natural things, but rather for a purely economic purpose, to provide water for the steam locomotives dispatched from a nearby railroad yard. Nonetheless, strenuous efforts were made from the beginning to maintain the lake and its surroundings in a natural state. When economic interests again intervened many years later, a coalition succeeded in preventing privatization and construction in the area. Thus, without simply having come about and developed by nature, the lake and its surroundings have become a place where nature thrives. Here nature rules almost entirely, and natural living things abound: oaks, hickories, and maples; geese, ducks, and all manner of birds; deer and bobcat; turtles, frogs, snakes, and fish of many sorts. Only the narrow, winding road and trails, the cottage that houses the caretaker, and the earthen dam betray

Painting of Radnor Lake (in Fall) by L. Linebaugh.
Gift to the author from David Wood.

that human intervention has played a role in forming and maintaining the lake and its surroundings. More and more that role has become one of preventing and effacing intervention so as to preserve the bounty with which nature has endowed this rare place.

In winter, however, much of this bounty is held in reserve, the vibrant life of the place withdrawn into a temporary simulation of death.

There was scarcely a ripple on the surface of the water. The sky was heavily overcast, and though noon was approaching there were only the barest of reflections to be seen on the water. Shrouded from view by the thick clouds, the sun cast no shadows. On the lake and around it there were at this time of year hardly any signs of life to be seen. The glorious colors of autumn had long since faded, and the dry leaves heaped up on the floor of the forest showed not a trace of the brilliance that had shone only a few weeks earlier. The bare trees were like skeletons left over from a former life. In this southern climate there was little hope even that snow would come to soften the look of winter. On the trees there was not yet even the slightest hue of the green that in early spring would announce— at least to those with some imagination—all that would come in the progress toward summer. There were no manifest signs of nature's true past or of its likely future.

And yet, even here, even in the dead of winter (as we call it), memory prevails, memory of what has come and gone again and again, memory turned around into anticipation of what is to come, of what, again and again, will come. It is because of this reversal of memory that there is hope even during the dead of winter, that even in the desolate time spring is already on the horizon. This memory and its reversal have nothing to do with the mere repetition of arbitrary sequences of signals; rather it is a memory that belongs to our most basic comportment to nature, a memory fitted to nature and to its times of abundance and of desolation.

Thus nothing is more natural than that we should long for memory also of ourselves. Nothing is more compellingly suggested by nature than that we should be capable of recalling whence we came and of reversing this memory into anticipation—or at least hope—as to whither we will go. Stories abound that both tell of and enact such memory and its reversal into hope. There are institutions founded on such memory, institutions that institute it and come to guarantee it, institutions that have endured for millennia. On the other hand, those who side with knowledge will take distance from the myths and will break with the institutions that enforce them. They will attest to abysmal ignorance regarding the whence and the whither of human beings, and they will summon the courage to confront the possibility that outside birth and death there is nothing and that within these limits we are simply abandoned to ourselves. They will insist on thinking the whence and the whither only as limits of human existence rather than filling the space of ignorance with mere fancies—assuming, as they do, that fancy has not the least thing to do with knowing, that knowing requires even the exclusion of imagination.

Yet not even the philosopher himself could resist telling such stories. As Socrates was about to go to his death, indeed as the very last speech that he would deliver to his closest friends assembled in his prison cell, he told a story about the place to which human souls would go after death, representing this place—most remarkably—as the true earth.

4
Arches

Paestum

16 March 1993

I headed down the coast from Naples, driving past Mt. Vesuvius and the ruins of ancient Pompei, on toward Salerno, bound for Paestum. My map indicated that just past Salerno the main road would turn almost due east away from the sea. Another road would go off almost in the opposite direction and wind along the Amalfi coast toward Sorrento, from which the ferries sail to Capri. There was also a third road, indicated on the map as a very minor route; it ran south right along the coast down to Paestum, then on through Agropoli to Velia.

I knew that in ancient times both Paestum and Velia had stood over-looking the sea, though the present-day shoreline lies some distance from each. Proximity to the sea would most certainly have been decisive for the sanctuary sites and for the temples and other edifices erected on these sites. Indeed one of the three great temples at Paestum has traditionally been called the Temple of Poseidon, though research has shown that this temple was most likely dedicated to Hera.

Though the road from Naples turned inland for a while, when I reached Salerno I again caught sight of the sea. It was then that I recalled visiting the Temple of Poseidon at Sounion several years earlier on my first trip to Greece. I could still picture the way the temple had been erected on a mass of stone jutting out into the Aegean, set there at the extremity of the land as a place for the god who shone forth from the sea, with the sea, as the sea. I remembered, too, standing there amidst the ruins of the temple, feeling the cool breeze blowing from the sea, bringing the scent of the sea, bringing also some relief from the heat of the blazing sun. Never would I forget the sight of the sea far below, which shone with a blueness more beautiful than I had imagined possible.

Thus it was that at Salerno I took the narrow, unimproved road that ran along the coast to Paestum. I knew that from the sanctuary at Paestum it was not possible even to get a view of the sea, much less to look out upon it as in antiquity; so it would be best to drive slowly along the coastal road, stopping occasionally when the view of the sea was especially spectacular. I proceeded, intent upon gathering some sense of the sea, of this particular expanse of sea, so as to bring it to the experience of the edifices in Paestum. Yet to my amazement the surface of the water could hardly be seen at all, not even as I drove or stood right beside it. Its virtual invisibility was not, however, a matter of its being blocked from view; rather, the water's surface remained largely unseen because under the blazing sunlight it sparkled so brilliantly that it was like a mirror reflecting no things at all but only pure light.

This was not my first visit to Paestum. A few years earlier I had seen the sanctuary for the first time. When one first beholds the temples at Paestum, the sight can draw one beyond oneself, inducing a kind of ecstasy in which one is utterly captivated by what is beheld, captivated to the point of self-oblivion. Yet as one ponders these magnificent ruins, both imagination and memory come into play, imagination filling out the ruins, reconstructing the temples, and summoning the priestesses and people of Greek antiquity to attend to the rites celebrated at these sites where the presence of the gods themselves could be invoked, memory bringing to the scene what one has read about the temples, not only historical and archeological reports but also philosophical reflections linked to the temples and their site. On my first visit, there had come to mind especially a discourse that describes the compounded, reciprocal shining in which the temples are engaged. According to this discourse, the luster

Siren Gate, Paestrum. From A. C. Carpiceci and L. Pennino, *Paestrum and Velia: Today and 2500 Years Ago* (Edition Matonti Salerno, 1992), 18.

and gleam of the stone, itself shining forth only by the grace of the sun, brings the light of the day and the breadth of the sky to shine forth.

Now, as I returned to Paestum, this discourse remained somewhat in play, but also I had begun to elaborate another, independent discourse about the stone of the temples and had decided to supplement this discourse with photographs. It was imperative therefore to visit the sanctuary as early in the day as possible, not only to avoid the hordes of tourists who arrive long before noon but also in order to photograph the temples in the optimal light. Thus I had left Naples quite early and by mid-morning had finished photographing the temples. As the temples were by now somewhat familiar to me—to the extent that such works can ever become familiar—I turned my attention to some of the other edifices that were to be seen on the site.

One of these brought me around again to thinking about light and especially about the sky. It was the Siren Gate, located in the eastern wall.

It is somewhat remote from the other main edifices, and I had hardly noticed it on my first visit. The wall into which the gateway was set was constructed from squared stones assembled without use of mortar. What was striking about the gateway was the perfect arch by which it was formed. The arch itself was constructed from radial stones set together without mortar and held in place by the keystone at the very top. The arch was, in turn, set atop two vertical rows of squared stones that were continuous with the wall.

Such arches were neither so common nor so significant in Greek architecture as they later became with the Romans. Observing the Siren Gate in Paestum, I recalled another seen on my earlier visit when I had gone on to Velia, the city that the Greeks called Elea, most famous for its philosophers. In the ruins of the ancient city I had marveled at the Rose Gate, which is topped by a perfect arch made of eleven radial stones and extended into a vault under what probably served as a viaduct. It is a magnificent structure, virtually unparalleled in Greek architecture up through the fourth century B.C.

The view through the Rose Gate had been especially provocative; across a sparsely settled plain, mountains could be seen outlined against the sky. Now, as I observed the Siren Gate and others within the sanctuary at Paestum, I was struck by the affinity with the sky. There is an arching of the sky, an elemental arching that belongs to it and that the arch of architecture could be taken to imitate from afar. Yet because of the sky's unlimited recession and—apart from cloud formations and atmospheric distortions—its utter uniformity, the arching of the sky cannot be seen in the way that one can see—indeed can follow stone by stone—an architectural arch. It is primarily the horizon, the joining of sky to earth, that makes us aware of the arching. Moreover, as a vault can be formed by extending an arch in the dimension of depth, the sky has also the character of a vault. It is, in the traditional phrase, the vault of the heaven. It is also that by reference to which we experience height, that which is itself unlimited height, unlimited precisely through its recessive character. The wealth of metaphors built on the valorizing of height and of upward directionality generally reaches back to this elemental comportment.

Rose Gate, Velia (Elea). From A. C. Carpiceci and L. Pennino, *Paestrum and Velia: Today and 2500 Years Ago* (Edition Matonti Salerno, 1992), 121.

As, toward evening, I was driving back to Naples, the intense images of the things seen during the day began to recede, and I noticed how thoroughly the onset of evening was transforming the surroundings. Now the sea had become visible; it had lost the sheen of invisibility that the brilliant sunlight had cast over it earlier during the day. Though it still held some of the colors of sunset, it had begun to assume the appearance of the nocturnal sea. I pulled over, got out of the car, and began walking slowly by the sea, wondering about the famous Homeric epithet, wondering whether it was not the nocturnal sea that could more fittingly be called wine-dark. Stopping and looking up, I noticed that the first stars had appeared. A line from Hölderlin came to mind, from the late poem that begins: "In lovely blueness. . . ." The line is a question that Hölderlin poses in reference to God. It asks: "Is he manifest like the sky?" My own question began to take shape around the word *manifest,* in German *offenbar:* Just how is the sky manifest? Just how is it open to our apprehension? Above all, I wondered at the simplicity of its manifestness, wondered that its manifestness could be so simple, so open, and yet also so varied depending on the time of day, the season, the atmospheric conditions, and sometimes even conditions on the earth. I wondered, too, that for all its manifestness there could still arise a need for an artwork—an arch, for instance—that would let it be properly seen.

5
Welkin

Seefeld
Tirol
5 June 1993

It was like taking off into the blue. First I had to follow the winding road that leads very steeply from the Inn Valley up to the plateau. Then after a short drive I parked at the edge of the town and boarded a cable car, which, running far above the forests on the slope of the mountain, went up almost to the tree line. Then I took another, smaller cable car, which went almost to the crest of the mountain. At this height there was only sparse vegetation, and there was no sign of human presence except for the simple paths, which led off in two directions. One led up toward the crest and then back around to the station. The other went across the face of the mountain to a point where, if one had stamina enough, one could make the steep climb up to the Seefelder Joch. At such a height, there among mountain peaks, the elemental is predominant. A kind of natural reduction comes into play to concentrate one's attention, natural in the double sense that it is brought about by nature, by one's movement on a natural landscape, and that the reduction focuses attention precisely on nature, indeed on the elemental in nature, which tends to be passed over, taken for granted. At such a height everything else has been left below, not only the usual things and concerns with which humans are preoccupied but also the time that measures and segments the everyday.

Mountains above Seefeld

There, six thousand feet beyond man and time, there is nothing but the bare, rocky earth and the brilliant, blue sky.

Gazing across the peaks and up at the blue dome that canopies them, one would not readily admit that, as we know on other grounds, there is no such thing as sky. For its persistence in framing all experience of things—even if sometimes only implicitly, without being itself visible—attests that it is ever operative, even if it is itself not an existing thing. Can one even imagine what giving it up would require? To declare the sky a sheer nullity—assuming one understands what such a nothing could be—would entail virtually relinquishing the appearance of things as such. For it is preeminently the sky that grants appearance, not only the light in which things for the most part appear but also the very opening, the open expanse, in which things come to appear. And yet, though it is from the sky that illumination spreads across the expanse of appearing things, it seems—most remarkably—that the sky is most truly revealed precisely when it is not filled with light, that is, when it appears as the nocturnal sky. Such, at least, is what certain findings would attest, thus distinguishing the appearance of the sky from that of nearly everything else, from all the things that are concealed by darkness and revealed only in the light.

However that may be, the sky at which I marveled on that day in early summer was the deep blue sky of the Alpine midday. Not the least marvelous feature of the diurnal sky is that it has no depth, none whatsoever. Yet its lack of depth is not a matter of its being simply surface, for it is not surface at all. Rather it is sheer recession, absolute recession, as one might say in order to convey that it is absolved from depth precisely by its character as recessive. Sky recedes indefinitely, without being either depth or surface.

On the other hand, certain kinds of clouds have a manifest depth in the form of voluminosity. This character, perceptible from the ground, is readily confirmed if one flies through them. If the clouds are driven by wind, their movement, seen either from the ground or from the air, makes manifest by contrast the absolute immobility of the sky. This immobility is all the more manifest when seen from the mountaintop. Earth and sky constitute the frame in reference to which all movement occurs, but they themselves do not move; this anti-Copernican thesis would be displaced only if one constituted another frame outside that which frames ordinary terrestrial experience. But even then no mobility would be displayed by the sky. Naturally, one observes various movements in the sky; but the movements of the sun, the moon, the stars, and the clouds occur against the absolute immobility of the sky. They are movements in the sky, not movements of the sky.

Everything about the sky has to do with light, shining, radiance. All the changes that can be observed in the sky, all that are changes *of* the sky itself and not of things in the sky, are changes presented only to vision. They are changes of light, as in the change from the diurnal sky to the nocturnal sky, or they are changes in the color of the light, as at twilight.

One of the most remarkable features of the sky, a feature that it shares with all that is elemental, is that it is not given perspectively. In the apprehension of ordinary things, of trees and houses and even of birds in flight, these things are always seen from some spatial perspective, and to this perspective they show only a certain face; they appear in a certain profile that opens upon the thing as a whole but nonetheless is limited. From the mountaintop, looking out over the town, I see the roofs of the houses; but were I in the town standing directly across the street from a house, I would see it from the front rather than from above, and correspondingly it would present to my gaze its front rather than its roof. Any such thing will always be seen from somewhere and not from everywhere; that this is always the case expresses a structural necessity belonging to the appearance of things as such. Seen always from somewhere, things are always present only partially to my apprehension, present only in a profile.

The sky involves no such structure. To be sure, the sky can be wholly or partially blocked from view, for example, by clouds. Also, if, for instance, I were down on the plateau, one or more of the surrounding mountain peaks would block my view of the sky near the horizon. But such limitations are contingent: returning to the mountaintop, traveling beyond the mountains, or waiting for a cloudless day will allow me to observe the sky without obstruction. But no change of location and no degree of patience will allow me to perceive a thing otherwise than in a certain profile, otherwise than from a certain perspective to which the thing refuses to show itself completely. Circulating through a series of perspectives changes nothing essential.

On the mountain, time, too, is otherwise than in the town. In a sense it is more manifest, indeed by virtue of the predominance of the sky, since it is precisely in the sky that time is encountered in the most elemental way. But the time that counts on the mountain is neither that of everyday concerns nor that measured by a precise chronometer. It is the time of the arrival and departure of light, the time meted out by the sun as it traverses the sky, also the time of the gathering thunderstorm from which one needs shelter, also the time of night and of the beauty and terror of the nocturnal sky.

As I walked down the mountain, climbing over boulders deposited by some long-ago avalanche, treading along the path through the ever denser pine forests, wandering freely across the open meadows, the time that continued to guide me was that of the mountain. And the sense that I opened to all these things was enlivened by the specter of the sky.

6

Sublimities

Grand Canyon (North Rim), Arizona/
Bryce Canyon, Utah
17 May 1994

There are places where virtually everything is sublime. There are land-scapes where little more than a widely sweeping gaze is required in order to reveal unimaginable sublimities. Their revelation is always a singular discovery. It is not as though we have some notion of what it means for something to be sublime and then go looking for something that fits this notion. Rather, when something sublime is discovered, it is from the thing itself that we get whatever notion we have of the sublime. It is the singular thing that conveys its sublimity to us, that bespeaks its sublimity. Or rather, since sublimities often do not consist of singular things but rather—as with the great canyons of the American West—of assemblages irreducible to a collection of discrete, singular things, it is the singular spectacle that comes before us—that announces itself—as something sublime. Such a spectacle can teach us what sublimity is, yet this teaching is something that we must ever again relearn with every new sublimity encountered.

Perhaps most often it is the gigantic proportion, the great magni-tude, of what the spectacle presents that makes it appear sublime. The magnitude of such sublimities will be such as to dwarf by comparison everything set on a human scale; it will make the human—both human beings and all with which they concern themselves—seem insignificant and inconsequential. We minuscule creatures are humbled as we stand before shapeless mountain masses piled on one another in wild disarray or as we gaze out across the expanse of a great canyon prepared by geological upheavals and carved by the waters of a mighty river. The sight of sublimity wrenches from us a confession: how insignificant we are in the face of gigantic nature! And yet, it belongs to the encounter with sublimity that this confession also turns around into a question, reserving therefore a dimension in which, gigantic though it be, we would exceed nature. This is the riddle of the sublime: that sublime nature both exceeds and yet is exceeded by the human who encounters it and that this double exceeding belongs to the encounter itself. The riddle is not something to be dissolved; rather, its persistence is required for that of the sublime itself. Should one or the other moment of excess become dominant— for instance, by appeal to a dimension beyond nature and its evocative places—then the sublimity itself would have dissolved.

Sublimities are discovered, announce themselves as such to us. Yet discovering them is not a matter simply of passive observation; we do not discover sublimities in the same way that we discover that a thing is blue. Encountering a sublimity is not an experience that we simply undergo; rather it is an engagement in which we let a natural spectacle, which we could perhaps simply have observed passively, present itself as sublime. In order for a sublimity to be encountered as such, more than mere receptivity is required; imagination must come into play in the very apprehension of the spectacle. For it is only through imagination that the sheer presence of nature can be surpassed and nature's excess apprehended. Imagination is uniquely capable of oscillating between two operations in a way that holds them together; specifically, it can hover between serial apprehension of contiguous parts of the spectacle and holistic comprehension of the entire spectacle. It is somewhat like the process involved in trying to take in the sight of one of the great pyramids. One needs both to examine the series of individual stones that make up the pyramid and to grasp the pyramid as a whole—that is, one needs to carry on both of these operations to the point where they merge into a synthetic view of the pyramid. Such synthesis can prove difficult: if one stands far enough away to get a full view of the pyramid, one may not be able to discriminate and observe the individual stones, whereas if one is close by, it may be impossible to get a comprehensive view of the entire pyramid from bottom to top. Indeed such synthesis may prove impossible; it is precisely in the experience of such impossibility that one encounters a spectacle as sublime. In this experience a point is reached where any further advance in the serial apprehension of parts disrupts comprehension of the whole. Through this double bind in which imagination comes to be engaged, the spectacle proves to be such that it withdraws from the effort to grasp it completely and as a whole. The assemblage presented proves also to hold itself in reserve, to retreat from being made fully present. It is in this sense that sublime nature is boundless: not that it goes on and on like a merely additive—that is, bad—infinity, but that it cannot be bound by imagination, that it, rather, escapes, retreats. It is also in this way that it exceeds imagination, that it even does violence to imagination. But also, because imagination engages in the double operation up to the point where it breaks down, there is, through imagination, an experience of sublime nature's exceeding of imagination. It is in and through this experience that we let sublimity announce itself.

Yet in this experience, in the proven capacity to let sublimity announce itself, the other dimension is first opened, the dimension of our exceeding of sublime nature. This excess would lie, then, in whatever is required for this capacity. It is, therefore, in the analysis of this requirement that the riddle of the sublime would be genuinely taken up. Yet in order to sustain the riddle and hence sublimity too, the analysis would need to remain oriented to nature and its evocative places and to forgo every leap beyond.

In the case of mountains or of the great canyons, magnitude is primarily what counts; it is in their magnitude that they prove to exceed the grasp of imagination and thus come to appear sublime. Yet magnitude is not the only respect in which such excess can occur. Canonical theories of the sublime recognize also might or power as making such excess possible; thus they distinguish the dynamically sublime from the mathematically sublime. Thunderclouds gathering in the sky, accompanied by lightning, a volcano threatening to erupt with all its destructive power, or a hurricane with its threat of devastation—these are spectacles that can appear as dynamically sublime, though clearly in many such instances they border also on the mathematically sublime.

The typology needs not only to recognize instances in which these two kinds are mixed; it needs also to be extended to include other, quite different kinds of sublimities. For it is not solely through magnitude or power that a spectacle can prove to exceed imagination in the sense of withdrawing from full apprehension. Is the sublimity of the ocean, for instance, primarily a matter of the virtually unlimited extent—that is, the magnitude—of its surface? Is it not also linked to the ocean's purely fluid character and most conspicuously to its depth? And while the ocean may indeed display its enormous power in a storm and thus appear as dynamically sublime, can it not also appear sublime when its surface is quite tranquil?

If we consider the immense variety of natural spectacles, then it seems still more imperative to extend the range of the sublime. Bryce Canyon, for instance, is not manifestly unlimited either in magnitude or in power; at least that character that is striking and that could be said to render it sublime has to do neither with magnitude nor with power. Partly because it is not really a canyon at all—there is no river running through it—this feature can be encountered without any effort to comprehend it as a whole. What is striking about Bryce Canyon is that the rock formations are so perfect and so elaborate that one cannot imagine that they were carved by nature and not by a human artist. When, before these amazing formations, imagination is given its play, the spectacle cannot but appear sublime.

It is remarkable that all these sublimities belong to nature. Even the canonical theories of the sublime exclude from this domain both works of art and natural things, both of which are too determinate in their form and purpose. The sublime is to be discovered only in raw nature—or, more precisely, in elemental nature rather than things of nature.

Correspondingly, many sublimities display an elemental time. Such a time can be seen as one looks across a great canyon and surveys its various

Bryce Canyon, Utah. From Tully Stroud, *The Bryce Canyon Auto and Hiking Guide*
(Bryce Canyon Natural History Association, 1983), 17. Photograph by
Paul R. Johnson.

levels all the way down to the mighty river on the valley floor. Elemental
time can also be seen in the rock formations unimaginably carved by
nature in Bryce Canyon. This is a time remote from the time that governs
human concerns; it is a time of flowing water and, above all, of stone, a
lithic time.

7
Garden Time

Kyoto
8 April 1996

Time can adhere to a place. Such adherence may occur by repetition, by one's repeatedly being at a certain place at the same time. A person who repeatedly arrives at a certain place at noon may come to associate this place with arrival at noon. The adherence may indeed be so strong that arriving at this particular place at another time will seem strange. The strangeness will be enhanced to the extent that this other time of arrival is indicated not just by the hands of a clock but by a change, for instance, in the character of the light, for then the place of arrival will look different. If, instead of the usual noon arrival, the person arrives as the sun is just setting or after dark, the strangeness of the place at this time will weaken the adherence of noon to this place.

Time can also adhere to place in another way, in a way that, if given priority, puts in question the understanding of time and of place that is usually taken for granted. This other kind of adherence is brought about, as we say, by nature; indeed the connections that it establishes belong most elementally to nature as such. It is an adherence of time to certain places as they are determined neither through coordinates nor by the occupying things but rather by the elements and by concurrences of the elements. As adherent to uranic places, time is preeminently time of day, that is, the time of the arrival and departure of sunlight: it is dawn when sunlight appears there on the eastern horizon, and it is noon when the sun is there overhead. There is also the time of the seasons: it is winter when the sun's daily trajectory keeps it low in the southern sky, when the fields lie barren and fallow, when the snow comes. There is also tempestuous time when several elements come together in a certain way, wind, rain, thunder, and lightning.

The adherence of time to such places of the elements and the way in which this adherence determines the very character of certain times cannot but seem strange in relation to the usual conception of time. This conception pictures time as a sequence of points each of which represents a moment. Disengaged from place, the passage of time would consist in the movement from one point to the next. Thus it is supposed that time can be represented as a line, a continuous line, though this supposition introduces difficulties and, even among the ancients, gave rise to paradoxes: if time is a line, then its passage cannot consist in the movement from one point to the next, since on a continuous line there is no next point. More precisely, in the interval between one point P_1 and any other point P_2 that might be taken to be the next point, there is still another point P_3, which is thus more entitled to be considered next after P_1. But then in the interval between P_1 and P_3 there is still another point P_4, and so on *ad infinitum*. If a handicap race is pictured in these terms, then Achilles will never be able to overtake the tortoise. The representation of time as a series of points also broaches another difficulty, a kind of antinomy with respect to the passage of time. For it is impossible to say with assurance whether we move along the line from one moment to the next or whether we are stationary and the line moves so as to deliver to us one moment after another.

Yet even aside from these difficulties that have long disturbed the picture of time as a sequence of moments, of successive nows or presents, there is something in the experience of time that is overlooked by this picture. One need only listen to a brief musical melody and pay attention to the experience in order to recognize that the present moment is not a point at all. If one merely heard each note discretely, stigmatically, independently of the preceding and succeeding notes, one could never hear the melody as such. In order to hear the melody as a melody, one must both hold in one's awareness the previously sounded notes and also anticipate (within a certain range of possibilities) the notes that are still to be sounded. In other words, the present moment must be such as to open onto the immediate past and the immediate future. Some philosophers have gone still further and regarded this opening to past and future as the basic structure of time; thus the temporal character of human experience would consist not in moving through a succession of moments, not in remaining stationary while those moments stream by, but rather in standing out from the present into the past and future. It would consist in ecstasis, in ecstasy.

Without disputing these advances in the understanding of time, recognition of the adherence of time to elemental places goes still further toward overcoming the reduction of time to a sequence of interior moments. Such recognition brings time back into nature, into elemental nature. It shows how our standing out toward past and future links up concretely with our engagement in a world framed by nature.

These were some of the thoughts about time that I sought to convey in the lecture I had come to Kyoto to present. I undertook also to explore the relation between time and imagination, and therefore, taking *dream* as one of the poet's words for imagination, I couched my discourse in images and phrases drawn from *A Midsummer Night's Dream.* The bonding of time and imagination that the very title of the play announces I ventured also to demonstrate by showing an image of Monet's *Wheatstack in Sunlight.* In the lecture I wanted, above all, to say and to show how time can be drawn back to nature, how its adherence to places of the elements can be traced. Afterward I wrote the following note on the last page of the lecture: "This is the way to resolve the problem that Heidegger never quite resolves, not even, for instance, in developing his concept of horizonal schema, namely, the problem of the discontinuity between temporal horizonality and worldly horizonality." Stated more simply and without reference to this elaborated context, the problem was to show that by standing out toward past and future we also stand out toward the world of things and of nature.

Two views of Ryōanji Garden, Kyoto

The dry landscape gardens that I visited in Kyoto, especially that of Ryōanji, prompted still other thoughts about time and nature. Or rather, these gardens drew me into another receptiveness to time and nature.

The garden of Ryōanji goes back to the end of the fifteenth or the beginning of the sixteenth century. Little is known about how it was constructed, and there is dispute also as to who constructed it. At first encounter it may seem odd that this enclosure and others like it are considered to be gardens. There are neither trees nor shrubs in it, though the enclosing wall is low enough that the many trees just outside can be seen; the fact that from the location from which one would contemplate the garden many trees are visible outside the wall serves to render all the more conspicuous their absence from the garden. There are also no flowers or flowering plants in the garden; though at this date, early April, I could see only a few blooms in the woods beyond the wall, a profusion of blooms would no doubt have been visible there a few weeks later. In the garden there are also no ponds, no streams, in fact no water at all. While I was there, I saw no birds in the garden, and I was told that it was only very rarely that a bird wandered into the enclosure.

At first sight, then, the place may appear to be desolate and arid. A Japanese philosopher once suggested that it should be called a garden of emptiness rather than a dry landscape garden or a rock garden. The contrast is striking, the contrast with the lush arboretum outside and even with the weathered hues and patterns on the yellowish wall that separates the garden from the outside.

Most of the surface of the garden is covered with white gravel. The gravel surface is lineated longitudinally, the evenly spaced heavier lines indicating the span of the rake used to produce the pattern. I was told that monks rake the gravel every day. On two sides, including the side from which one contemplates the garden, there is a border of pebbles laid in a kind of sunken trough such that the surface is on the same level as the gravel surface. The pebbles are much larger and more rounded than the pieces of gravel, and they are gray, much darker than the gravel. Along with the wall they serve to demarcate the enclosure.

Otherwise the garden consists only of five groups of rocks, fifteen rocks in all; there are three groups toward one end of the garden, one toward the other end, and one placed midway near one edge. In each of the five groups there is one rock much larger than the others. Around each cluster of rocks there is an earthen area separating them from the white gravel. It is primarily on these areas that something living is to be seen, namely, a brownish-green moss; the color extends onto some of the rocks as a thin layer of lichen. The moss is much more conspicuous in some other, similar gardens such as that of Ryōgenin, though the basic pattern is the same: rocks surrounded by an earthen, mossy area, surrounded by a surface of white, raked gravel. Except for these small bits of green, the entire garden is devoid of life.

Yet the rocks are as in nature. Their irregular natural shapes have not been altered. Though little is known in detail about the construction of the garden, one rule is known: the rocks must not be shaped by human hands nor in any way altered from their natural condition. Thus they are set up in the garden precisely as they were formed by nature, precisely as they were sculpted by water and more indirectly by the earth itself. Hence these most prominent sights in the garden attest to the workings of nature across the great expanse of lithic time. They stand in the garden as the works of nature and time.

Only the rocks rise above the surface of the garden. It is as though they had erupted through the white gravel surface, exposing almost bare earth in the area adjacent to them. As they stand protruding above the surface, they present the upward thrust of the earth itself. Indeed it is primarily in the guise of rock, as stone, that the earth—otherwise and even still self-withholding, unpresentable as such—comes to be present.

Mimetic thoughts readily come into play as one contemplates the garden, thoughts that seek to match what is beheld there by matching the spectacle mimetically with something else. Then one will say that the rocks are like mountains, the clusters of rocks like mountain ranges, and the graveled surface like an expanse of water, like the sea. Yet the mimetic doubles assembled in—or rather, as—the garden are separated from nature, the rocks detached, the sea dried up. Precisely as they bring nature into the garden, they are secluded from nature, even literally cut off by the wall and the trough of gray pebbles. Nature is brought into the garden just as fresh blooms are preserved in the guise of dried flowers. Like dried flowers, the garden presents the working of nature and time by arresting it.

It is imperative to remain in the garden for a long time, for a time long enough to erase one's memory of how long one has been there, long enough to instill an obliviousness to the measure of time. What counts, instead, is the way in which this place not only stills the workings of time but also transmutes time, even suspends the flow that otherwise seems to be time itself. Mimetic thoughts, too, will be suspended. As one contemplates the garden, one comes to see that the things that compose it—the protruding rocks, the exposed, mossy earth, the white gravel surface bordered by the wall and the gray pebbles—are not like anything, that they are just themselves. As Nishitani once said, each is an image without an original.

The garden is a place to which time adheres in a unique way, in such a way that its workings in nature are presented precisely in being stilled, as, at the same time, the one who admires the garden is set free in the suspension of time's flow.

8

Islands

Tinos

22 June 1998

What attracts us to Greece is its history, not in the sense of a continuous development up to the present, but in the sense that once, in antiquity, an origination took place for which, up to the present, a measure is still lacking. Yet, once we are there—at least at certain places in Greece—not only history but also the nature with which that history is bound up proves uncommonly engaging. Indeed it can—in certain places—engage us even beyond its bond to the originary history of Greece.

If one comes directly from northern Europe, especially if, traveling by air, one is abruptly translated to this wholly other landscape, it will at first seem exceedingly barren. Even if one is returning to Greece and not visiting for the first time, the impression one gets from the mountains around Athens is that of a bleak and desolate land exposed to too much sun and relieved by too little rain. The smooth contours and soft colors of the northern forests and fields, which one will still have in mind after the abrupt transposition to Greece, are nowhere to be seen. There are only the bare mountains, scorched by the blazing summer sun, apparently devoid of living vegetation. Continuing along the main artery into Athens, one sees nothing distinctive except the Greek script, which to anyone occupied with ancient Greek texts seems rather out of place when seen

Acropolis, Athens

on street signs and on the facades of buildings. Nothing is to be seen that in any way makes present the antiquity, the originary history, in search of which one will have come to Greece. On the contrary, the scene is that of a modern city with all the typical ills, though in this case amplified by the climate and the economic underdevelopment. There are too many cars, too much noise, and too much pollution in the air, yet there is almost none of the architectural beauty that redeems such cities as Paris and Chicago.

Only when the Acropolis comes into view in the distance, set apart above the city, does one get a first glimpse of that history that has brought one to Greece. Though one knows that even there above the city the noise and pollution will not be entirely absent, the very way in which the Acropolis appears gives it the look of something other, makes it look as though it belonged to a world quite other than that of the modern city. For it appears as though it were an island floating above the city, offering refuge to those who would escape the imminent dangers lurking in the rapid currents swelling around it. It not only appears to float above the modern city, but also, precisely thereby, it interrupts the space of the modern city. Within that space, at the very center, it opens upon that other world, the world of originary Greek history. For in the ruins atop the Acropolis, that history has left a legible trace. Once the Acropolis has been seen, once the traces have begun to congeal into an outline of that other world, the interruptive force spreads throughout the city so that every place— regardless of whether it affords a view of the Acropolis—will be haunted by the specter of these remains of antiquity. It will be as if the Acropolis hovered over the entire city or as if, like the rocky coast of an island, it not only withstood the force of the waves but also deflected them back across the sea.

But it is necessary to leave Athens in order to experience nature in a way that goes beyond the first impression. If one sets out to reenact such experiences of nature as were taken up into the poetry and thought of the ancients—most notably, the poetry of Homer and the thought of the so-called Presocratic philosophers—then the best course is no doubt to sail as soon as possible to the islands. For in the Homeric epics the sea and the islands are ever present; and among the early philosophers those who did not live on islands—as Pythagoras lived on Samos and Empedocles on Sicily—resided in cities situated on the sea, such as Miletus, Ephesus, and Elea. The sea was ever present, and the air that inspired Greek poetry and thought was that of the sea.

From Athens we traveled by bus to the port city of Rafina, situated on the east coast of the Greek mainland and thus much closer to the Cyclades than Piraeus. At Rafina we boarded a hovercraft, which sped us out to Tinos in only a couple of hours. It was there, in Tinos, that we boarded the small ship that over the next week would transport us to several islands in the Cyclades chain. The ship was only thirty-three meters in length. It had a single mast and could be driven by sails, though nowadays, so I was told, it was nearly always powered by its three relatively small engines. The ship had a crew of five, and there would be twelve passengers aboard. Nights

Dovecotes on Tinos

were spent on the ship, mornings were spent sailing from one island to the next, and the remaining time was spent ashore.

The day after our arrival from Athens was spent visiting the sights in Tinos. We set out early, traveling by bus around the island and up into the mountains to the ancient acropolis. By now the images of green, fertile countryside brought along in memory from northern Europe had begun to fade, and thus our senses became more open to the beauty of the stark, almost treeless island landscape around us. The most unusual sight, one distinctive of Tinos, was that of elaborate dovecotes. There were hundreds of them, some so elaborate that our guide described them as artworks. For some of us the dovecotes evoked a familiar image as well as an extension of this image. The image pictures a dove that, feeling the resistance of the air, soars upward, supposing that in empty space its flight would be still easier. The implication is that, like human thought, the dove will not succeed in soaring beyond the atmosphere, that it will not escape the draw of the earth. Despite its capacity for flight, the dove is bound to be housed on the earth. Its bond to the earth is set into place in and as the dovecotes.

I read one account according to which the highest peak on Tinos, Mt. Tsiknias, was the mythical abode of the wind god Aeolus. If credence is accorded to this account, then Tinos would be identified as the floating island on which, according to the *Odyssey,* Aeolus lived. The Homeric account is that when Odysseus asked Aeolus about the way home and requested conveyance, the god gave him a bag made of oxhide and stuffed with all the blowing winds; for Aeolus had been appointed by Zeus to be in charge of the winds. The bag was put in the ship, and the west wind alone was set free to carry Odysseus and his men home. And they would have reached Ithaca had it not been for the folly of the crew. For, as they came within sight of their homeland and Odysseus was overcome by sleep, his men opened the bag, thinking that it contained silver and gold. The winds all burst out, and the storm swept the ship away from their country and back to the floating island. But now Aeolus would offer no further assistance, and Odysseus and his crew were forced to sail on, unaided.

We, too, were vexed by the winds. The plan had been to spend only the first day in Tinos and on the morning of the second day to sail on to Mikonos. But the winds were so high and the sea consequently so rough that our small ship could not set sail. We spent the day mostly wandering around Tinos City, visiting the church and the stalls full of religious paraphernalia that lined the street leading up to the church—all of it pure overlay, manifesting nothing of the originary history of Greece, disconnected, too, from the expanse of nature to be seen on the island.

On the third day the winds were still too high for our ship to sail, and we were beginning to fear that we would be stranded for the entire week on this floating island. But, fortunately, arrangements were made for us to take a day trip to Mikonos on a much larger ship. Arriving on Mikonos, a few of us then slipped aboard another vessel that, after a very rough half-hour ride, landed us on Delos for a couple of hours. This gem of the Cyclades shone like the wonder it had been in antiquity when it was one of the most sacred places in Greece. Still today, walking along

Two views of Delos

the sacred way, reconstructing in imagination the temples once erected to Apollo here on the island of his birth, looking out over the sacred lake where, even though it is now filled in, one can picture to oneself the beautiful swans sacred to Apollo, and standing before the magnificent archaic lions just across from the lake, one can sense something of the ancient sacredness of the place. On this small island of only one square mile, where the sea is ever in view and the sunlight is almost blinding in its intensity, the gods could become present for the ancients, not only Apollo and Artemis, to whom the island was especially sacred, but also Poseidon, Hermes, Dionysus, and Zeus himself; there is even a terrace of the foreign gods, built on Mt. Kynthos for the shrines of non-Greek deities. On this island, still maintained today as a sanctuary without any human inhabitants other than caretakers, the gods could become present: for instance, at the Delian festival, organized every four years by the Athenians and consisting of processions of pilgrims crowned with flowers who came to sacrifice oxen, to take part in sacred dances, and to compete in drama and sport. Being there on Delos, even today, one realizes that its sacredness had nothing to do with the otherworldly piety of later religion. It was a sacredness that inhered in nature itself rather than referring beyond nature. For it was in and from nature—in and from the sea, the earth, the sky—that the gods appeared, even when they became present in the temples erected to honor and to house them.

What could have been a rather uneventful excursion of a few hours to Mikonos was thus exchanged for an intense experience of a place where much that belonged to the originary history of Greece was gathered in its relation to elemental nature.

All too soon we were under way back to Mikonos and then to Tinos. Our journey proper had still not begun as we remained in Tinos on the evening of the third day, still captives, it seemed, of Aeolus.

The spectacle of an island and perhaps even more the fantasy of a floating island prompt thoughts about the earth and the sea and about their way of belonging together. In a sense sea is the opposite of earth: the sea as such offers no support, and this is why humans must fabricate ships if they are to venture upon the sea. On the other hand, the earth is all-supporting, to such an extent that other supportive things fabricated by humans (houses, for instance) borrow support from the earth. Yet the sea and the earth are not merely opposites; the sea belongs to the earth, even dividing and articulating its surface. The sea is an opposite that belongs intimately to the earth: as when a relatively small expanse of earth is surrounded by sea and seems even to float upon it.

When we awoke on the fourth day, our entreaties to Aeolus had been answered. There was no wind, and the sea was perfectly calm. At last our ship set sail.

9

Caldera

Sailing on the Aegean
to and from Santorini
24 June 1998

On Santorini it is nature rather than history that draws one's interest. The island now has the shape of a crescent. Archeologists have shown that it assumed its present shape as a result of a volcanic eruption some three and a half millennia ago. The eruption left a huge central crater, which filled up with seawater. Its ashes buried the town of Akrotiri, a highly developed Minoan city, now excavated and quite remarkable to behold. Many believe that the resulting tidal wave that would have swept south to Crete is what destroyed the Minoan civilization on that island.

There is also a story often taken to have been set on Santorini, the story of Atlantis. This is the story that Critias tells in Plato's *Timaeus,* a story that Critias declares was passed down to him ultimately from Solon, to whom it was told by a priest in Egypt. Much of the story is actually about the wisdom and courage of the ancient Athenians, who defeated the invaders from Atlantis. After this defeat, so the story goes, the island of Atlantis sank beneath the sea and vanished—just like the caldera of Santorini. On the other hand, the story does not quite square with this identification. For in the *Timaeus* Atlantis is described as being located in front of the Pillars of Hercules, and the inhabitants of Atlantis are

Santorini

contrasted with those who live within the boundaries of Hercules, that is, around the Mediterranean.

Yet, even aside from the story, there is perhaps no site in Greece that is more dramatic than the one beheld as one sails into the caldera. It is bounded on the side of the island by a high cliff atop which is the main town of the island. On the seaward side are three much smaller islands. As, having landed, one makes one's way up the narrow path, either on foot or by donkey, finally reaching the town above, the view over the caldera and the smaller islands presents a spectacle so rare that one will likely remain silent for some time, living entirely in one's perception, lacking words fitting to what one sees.

Even as, some hours later, our ship sailed out of the caldera and headed north across the Aegean, my sight remained captive to the island until finally it disappeared, this monument to the power of the earth erected by this very power. This power, when it erupted in the distant past, shaped the island into a graphic trace in which one can sense this ancient event. Such events, volcanic eruptions and also earthquakes, belong intimately to the earth; they are events in which the earth displays its gigantic power. On the other hand, they belong to the earth as opposites, for they suspend the support and security provided by the earth as such. Whereas the earth supplies nourishment for all things and lets them flourish in conditions of stability, volcanic eruptions and earthquakes are destructive of life as such and of the conditions that sustain it.

10

Thalassic Surfaces

Compared to most other Greek islands, Samos appears lush and green. It boasts extensive vineyards from which comes the sweet Muscat wine for which the island has long been known. The town that now occupies part of the site of the ancient city of Samos was renamed in modern times and is now called Pythagorio. The eastern tip of the island lies a little more than a mile from the Turkish coast. Ships run regularly to the Turkish town of Kusadasi, and from there it is only a short distance north to the archeological site of Ephesus. A bit farther to the south along the Turkish coast and less easily accessible is the archeological site of the ancient city of Miletus.

The triangle formed by the three ancient cities, Samos, Ephesus, and Miletus, marks one of the primary places where philosophy originated and was furthered in its originary guise. In the city now named for him, Pythagoras was born; he is reported to have been living there still around 532 B.C., though later he emigrated to Croton in southern Italy. According to Iamblicus' *Life of Pythagoras,* Pythagoras was the first to call himself a philosopher, understanding by this name one who devotes himself to the contemplation of the most beautiful things. Pythagoras reportedly declared that the whole heaven and the stars that revolve therein are among the most beautiful things because of their order, because they partake of number. According to another account, by Diogenes Laertius, Pythagoras compared the philosopher to one who comes to a festival as a spectator, who seeks only to see and not to promote his fame or gain. This practice of vision, this adherence to the spectacle, was thus primary in determining the very sense of philosophy in its originary history, even when, as in the Pythagorean community, this practice issued in an advocacy of number as origin. Porphyry's *Life of Pythagoras* attests that Pythagoras was held in the highest esteem even by Empedocles, who likely would have had word of him after his emigration to southern Italy. Empedocles' formulation indicates that what he found praiseworthy and identified with the work of wisdom was precisely the practice of vision: "There was among them a man of immense vision, who had acquired the greatest wealth of understanding and who was masterly in all sorts of wise works."

Across the narrow strait separating Samos from the mainland, in the city of Ephesus, at almost the same time, Heraclitus pursued this practice that Pythagoras had named philosophy. Among the fragments of Heraclitus' writings passed down by later authors, there are several that mention Pythagoras, sometimes critically ("Much learning does not teach intelligence; otherwise it would have taught . . . Pythagoras"), sometimes appreciatively ("Pythagoras practiced inquiry beyond all men"). With Heraclitus, too, despite all that issues from it, the practice is one of adherence to things as they appear, as they become manifest. Thus one especially significant fragment contains the following self-description: "I distinguish each thing according to nature and declare how it is." Another fragment says that wisdom is "to speak and do the truth, apprehending things according to nature." Still another indicates the guise taken by such apprehension of things. In an extended translation it can be rendered: "The man who is most esteemed, who most appears wise, is one who knows, that is, keeps watch over and preserves, that which appears."

Directly south from Ephesus along the coast of the mainland, in the city of Miletus, a few decades earlier, those traditionally considered the very first Greek philosophers were active, their practice antedating even the word. At least we have it on the testimony of Simplicius, writing a millennium later, that Thales was the first to have revealed the investigation of nature to the Greeks; other later writers attest that Anaximander and Anaximenes were also active in Miletus at about the same time. In these philosophers not yet called philosophers, there is a trace—so far as the scant records allow us to discern—of a practice consisting in the watchful adherence to that which appears. According to Aristotle, Thales proposed that the earth floats on water, which he took to be somehow the origin of things. If one sets out of action the Aristotelian grid that compels one to see in this proposal only a thesis about the material constitution of things, then there is reason to think that Thales' proposal was not the senseless fantasy that later philosophers would take it to be but rather that it results from a practice of adhering to what appears, to what is manifest. For what is more manifest—what would have been more manifest to a philosopher at this originary site on the sea—than that the world consists of water (of seas) in which various expanses of earth are set? As with islands. As with the floating island that Aeolus was said to inhabit.

We came by ferry from Rhodes. It was a very small ferry. There was only one sitting room, and except for the two of us, everyone aboard was Greek; several of the passengers were ordinary folks who were sailing out to the islands to sell the goods they had brought along. On the ferry we sat almost at the level of the sea's surface, especially in the open space at the back of the boat, which became my observation post. The boat's engine was noisy, and outside the cabin one constantly smelled the fumes from the engine. Yet it was as though the blocking of these senses, which otherwise are revelatory of the sea, served to concentrate and make more perceptive the vision of the sea. Abstracting from the other senses, one could live entirely in one's vision.

From Rhodes we sailed almost due west to Kos and then to Kalimnos, discharging passengers, many of them burdened down by their wares, and taking on a few more, mostly people whose features and dress made them look as though they belonged to these islands. From Kalimnos we headed north, stopping briefly at Patmos, then passing the site of Miletus, not accessible by ferry, and finally arriving, after several hours under way, at Pythagorio. Our stay on Samos was to be punctuated by excursions to

Aegean surface

archeological sites on the Turkish mainland. As the magnificent ruins—especially in Ephesus—evoked the originary history of Greece, so the surface of the sea, apprehended in a practice of vision, evoked something of the nature bound up with that history.

The surface of the sea is doubly reflective. As soon as one's vision opens receptively to it, one will observe that it is not merely surface, that in its very way of appearing, the surface of the sea makes manifest the hidden depth below, that it makes this hidden depth manifest without betraying its hiddenness. At the same time, opening one's vision to the surface, one will observe that the surface of the sea is overlaid with a play of shinings and reflections; on a day when there is intense sunshine, these shinings and reflections on the surface of the sea may virtually conceal the surface itself, so that one sees the shinings and reflections on the surface but not the surface itself.

Sunset on the Aegean

Observing both the reflection of the surface into the hidden depth and the shinings and reflections that, on the surface, conceal that surface, one will also be drawn into reflection, no longer remaining receptively oriented to a merely present surface but reenacting in one's own reflection the double reflection that breaks up the presumed mere presence of the surface. Once such reflection sets in, other elements too will be traced in their connection with the sea.

One will reflect, for instance, on the darkness of the sea. The way in which the surface of the sea glistens and is broken up by whitecaps only serves by contrast to bring out the darkness of the sea. Along the course we took going north toward Samos, the sea was such a deep blue, almost blue-black, that it made the blue of the sky look almost washed out, even though the day could not have been clearer nor the sky more blue. One observes also how fragile the color of the sea surface can be: when churned up by the boat, the sea surface acquired, in the wake, a streak of bright aqua across the very deep blue.

One notices also how thoroughly the color of the sea is determined by the sky and the sun. At sunset the surface of the sea was almost entirely red, reflecting the brilliant color of the western sky as the sun transmuted into a fireball perched on the horizon. What was most remarkable was that the thalassic surface remained red, hardly changing at all, for quite a long time after the sun had set. It continued to hold the sun's color even after the sun had long since sunk beneath the horizon. Only as night settled in did it again become, in Homer's phrase, the wine-dark sea.

11

Lightlines

Sani, Halkidiki
Macedonia
7 July 1998

In Thessaloniki we were hardly aware of the sea, even though the city is situated directly on the gulf named for it and is the major port in northern Greece. But the stifling heat, the noise, and the fumes in the city made us think of the sea only as a distant respite reserved for future days, and even when we caught a glimpse of the water in the harbor it seemed strangely unlike itself. For the time being we slipped into another way of inhabiting the day, letting it stretch toward the evening, when finally, not long before midnight, we could dine outside in the cool night air.

Thessaloniki is located at the northern edge of the Halkidiki peninsula, which extends like a three-fingered hand from the northern coast of Greece into the Aegean. Halkidiki is known for its monasteries, its charming seaside villages, and an important archeological site; two of the three smaller peninsulas that extend beyond the main peninsula are especially well suited to offer relief to those fleeing the heat and all that goes with it in the city. On these two peninsulas there are deep pine forests, fields of wheat, groves of olive trees, and fine sandy beaches.

Our Greek friend, a professor at the Aristotle University of Thessaloniki, had promised us a day in Sani, where she had a summer house only a short walk from the beach. A few years earlier she had taken us there for

a few days, and ever since, we had cherished fond memories of this idyllic place. To be sure, there were some signs of encroaching tourism to be
seen, but around her summer house set deep in the pine woods they were
entirely absent. Even on the nearby beach they had not yet become intru-
sive. Nearly everyone there appeared to be Greek.

We drove almost due south from Thessaloniki across the main peninsula of Halkidiki, then turned eastward for a few kilometers before turning
back south onto the peninsula of Kassandra, the westernmost of the three
smaller peninsulas. As we crossed over the canal that breaches the isthmus
at the site of the ancient city of Poteidaia, the sea made its appearance:
it became visible on both sides of the narrow isthmus, which forms the
northernmost segment of the peninsula of Kassandra; and, at the same
time, it came to presence in all that the name Poteidaia calls up, even in
the very name itself, which derives from the Doric variant of *Poseidon*.
After driving south for a while along the peninsula, we turned off the
main road and proceeded westward to Sani.

The day was clearer than I could ever have imagined possible. There
were no clouds, only uniformly blue sky without any differentiation other
than the brightening around the sun. There was not the slightest trace of
fog or mist or haze, and so, looking directly westward from Sani across the
bay, we could see Mt. Olympus distinctly contoured against the sky. Even
on the horizon the blue of the sky remained absolutely the same, utterly
uniform. A comment to our Greek friend about the remarkable blue of
the sky set off a conversation about the way in which both the blue of the
sky and the blue of language, the blue that can be said in the word *blue,* are
unlimited. This was clear enough in the case of the sky: its blue was not
interrupted by anything whatsoever, so that wherever there was sky, there
was one and the same blue, self-identical, selfsame blue. Furthermore, the
blue of the sky did not appear as the blue of a surface behind which something else might come to limit it; the sky is no surface at all but unlimited
regression, as is, too, its blue. Yet what fascinated me was the connection
that our friend, hearing English with a Greek ear, drew between the unlimited blue of the sky and that of the word. The word *blue,* she observed, is
unlimited because it has no terminating phoneme; there is no sound that

brings it to an end, but rather one can extend the word almost indefinitely (blu—) without altering its signification.

Yet it was not even in the blue of the sky that the light proved most remarkable. As we went out into the water, we swam a little but mostly just stood, up to our waists in the water, and marveled at the phenomenon we witnessed. Whether our Greek friend had seen it before I do not know, but for us it was an absolutely unique spectacle. As in much of the Aegean, the water was almost purely transparent; but also it was bright, not just on the surface where it reflected the sunlight but rather throughout its depth, which at that point was just over a meter. It seemed not just to reflect the light from its surface but to be completely infused with the light. Toward the bottom, though not precisely at the bottom, there were multiple extremely bright lines of light. These lightlines formed a network in the water, and this network of light was constantly mobile, shifting to one side and then to another. The sunlight was literally tracing the pattern of lightlines in the water, and the water was conveying its movement to the lightlines. In this remarkable phenomenon, light and water entered into an intimacy unimaginable except in such a place.

As the sun blazed overhead and we stood engulfed by the lightlines undulating with the sea, looking out also at Mt. Olympus in the distance, our host turned to me and asked whether this was not indeed a fitting time for me to tell her about what I had just written about Plato's *chora*.

12

Ascent

Soglio
Graubünden
15 July 1998

Not all thoughts are alien to places. Not all are such that thinking them requires disregarding the particular place where one happens to be at that moment. Not all thoughts can be thought just as readily in one place as in another. Not all are such that they can be thought—indeed with the same clarity and intensity—anywhere. Not all thoughts require a thinking elevated above and beyond everything local and concrete. If, especially in our time, thought is no longer taken as engagement with a utopian intelligibility, then its bond to certain things and places will be allowed to come into play. Hence Nietzsche could tell the story of the arrival of a thought. He relates that he was walking around Lake Silvaplana and that near Surlei he approached a large pyramid-shaped rock beside the lake. It was here, Nietzsche attests, that the idea of the eternal return came to him.

Today every philosophical pilgrim to Sils Maria has retraced this path and beheld the large pyramid-shaped rock beside the lake. Though perhaps anyone who has read *Thus Spoke Zarathustra* carefully can sense that it belongs somehow to this setting, that it breathes the very air of this place, it remains to be said what this singular event recounted by Nietzsche signifies. How is it that thoughts arrive, that they come as if from nowhere and yet arrive precisely as one comes to a certain place? How is it that their arrival is linked to a certain place? Even granted that thoughts do come—that they are not merely produced—is their coming pertinent to what is thought thereby? Or is the link to a certain place to be set aside as something quite accidental? It must be admitted that putting in play such ancient, now almost effaced, concepts does not advance the question. For the idea in question is that of the eternal return, and one consequence of this idea is that it disturbs the classical differentiation between the necessary and the accidental or contingent. When the idea comes, it will already have disrupted the possibility of dismissing its coming as merely accidental.

Can the significance of thought's coming at a certain place be rigorously determined? How would thought come to carry out such determination? Or does the happening of thought remain always elusive?

When we retraced the way around Lake Silvaplana and saw the large pyramid-shaped rock, we were in fact on an afternoon excursion, taking a side trip to this already familiar place from the town that had been our primary destination. There, in Soglio, we had taken lodging at the 350-year-old Palazzo Salis—now a hotel—and had spent several days wandering in the magnificent Bergell Mountains in the midst of which Soglio is situated. The family for which the palazzo is named has been prominent in the canton of Graubünden for centuries. According to accounts I found at the hotel, the family originally came from the area around Como in the tenth or eleventh century; indeed from Soglio it is only a few kilometers to the Italian border. I discovered also that the spelling of the family name had varied, and the disclosure that on the French-speaking branch of the family the *L* had sometimes been doubled spurred on the phantasy of origins that had attracted me to Soglio in the first place.

I read a good bit about Meta von Salis, who was the first woman in Switzerland to be awarded a doctorate and who was a close friend of Nietzsche's, often mentioned in his letters. In the summer of 1887 she spent six weeks in Sils Maria, and Nietzsche mentions going on walks with her. She was there again in August 1888, and in a letter to his mother Nietzsche recounts having gone boating with her around Lake Silvaplana.

In a letter to Köselitz dated 9 December 1888, Nietzsche reports that she gave him 1,000 francs for the printing costs for *The Twilight of the Idols*. Meta von Salis was among those to whom Nietzsche penned a letter in the days following his collapse in Turin. The letter, dated 3 January 1889, is one of the strangest. Nietzsche declares that since God is on earth, the world is transfigured. And he asks: Do you not see how all the heaven rejoices? Announcing that he has taken possession of his kingdom, Nietzsche signs the letter: The Crucified. A few years later Meta von Salis published a small monograph on Nietzsche in which she recounts her conversations with him and cites from other letters she received from him. Her admiration for Nietzsche and her sense of spiritual kinship with him is striking, for instance, in her description of him as the loneliest, proudest, and gentlest man of our century, living in the silent mountain world of the Upper Engadine like a prince born in exile.

Nothing is more thoroughly put into question in Nietzsche's thought than origins and the return to origins. The interrogation is radical: it is a question of the very sense of origin, of the sense (direction) of the return to origins, and, inseparable from these, a question of the origin of sense. Nietzsche deploys a variety of genealogies designed to show that the lower is the origin of the higher: that good originates from evil, intelligence from sense, truth from lies. Thus the turn to the lower constitutes no longer a falling away from the origin but precisely the return to the origin.

However, such inversion does not simply leave the governing opposition intact but, once followed through, destabilizes and displaces it. If truth originates from lies, from systematic falsifications that come to be taken for granted, then truth is none other than lie; truth is, then, as Nietzsche said, the kind of lie without which a certain kind of living being could not live. But if truth is just a kind of lie, then the difference between them will have been so effaced, so reduced, that neither can be put forth as origin of the other. Returning in either direction would, if taken as return to origin, be equally fanciful, regardless, too, of whether the return is construed as genealogy or as philosophy itself.

Now something else would be required, something quite beyond Nietzschean genealogy and the play of phantasy to which finally it too submits. Now there would be required sufficient force of imagination to turn sense back upon itself and let the very happening of sense, of manifestation, come to light. Such an ineluctably elusive origin would be, in the Platonic phrase, beyond being, even though sought in utmost proximity to sense. Precisely because of the demand for such proximity to sense, it could not but be sought at places that are distinctively evocative in their way of letting things become manifest. Such return to origin, adherent to place and to sense, could perhaps also be called a kind of phantasy of origins, though it is so other as to destabilize the very schema of division into kinds.

From the valley far below with the forests of fir and larch, we followed the narrow, winding road up to the shelf on which Soglio is situated. Nearly all the buildings in the town appeared ancient, consisting of rough-hewn stones and heavy timbers; some were plastered over, but many were not. The roofs were made of heavy overlapping slabs of slate. There were some flower boxes with red geraniums, though fewer than one saw farther north. At one point we came across a huge double outdoor tub filled with water and covered by a roof of the same style as those of the houses; this had once been, no doubt, the common laundry facility for the town. The spaces between the houses were so narrow that our small car could barely pass through on the sole street leading up through the village to the palazzo. All other passageways were for pedestrians only and in many instances were so narrow that only one person at a time could pass through them. The area around the palazzo was somewhat less crowded. The palazzo itself had a fine restaurant, with service in good weather in the lovely garden in the back. Though in need of some upkeep and remodeling, the palazzo still showed signs of its former grandeur.

But everything paled in view of the mountain peaks that soared above us on all sides. The narrowness and compactness of everything in the town stood in marked contrast to the way the mountains opened to the sky. And yet, the contrast was moderated, even transmuted, by a certain affinity between the human habitations and the natural splendor that soared above them. The affinity derived, first, from the peculiar antiquity of the houses, an almost timeless antiquity rather than a relation to a

Bergell Mountains above Soglio

bygone era, and, second, from their very rough, stony character, which was accentuated by contrast with the palazzo. There was something almost natural about these houses being set there at this site, and the sense of this almost natural placement was enhanced by contrast as I recalled the site of another Alpine town, Seefeld, where, a few years earlier, I had gone up into the surrounding mountains and had been engaged by the view afforded from there over the town. The antique, almost natural quality that Soglio displayed in its mountain setting had been lacking entirely in Seefeld, a relatively modern town built largely for purposes other than mere human habitation. Thus the stark opposition displayed by Seefeld, the opposition between the predominantly elemental in the mountains and the everydayness in the town below, proved to be muted and to a degree undermined by the affinity that Soglio had to its mountain setting. Soglio belonged there in the mountains, and both its character and its tempo gave the impression that it had somehow been left behind by

Mountains in the Engadine near Sils Maria

time itself, or rather that it had followed a course so different that it had fallen far behind, its very temporality mutating in the direction of lithic time, making it still more akin to the mountains themselves.

Yet still, the sight of the mountains around Soglio, of their magnificent peaks, was incomparable. What was most striking was that here we saw—outside all questions of return to origins and of genealogies capable of exposing origins—something unconditionally original, something beyond which, in interrogating things, one could not go, since all things have their site in the enclosure formed by earth and sky. In these elementals of nature, distinctively manifest in this place, we found what, though open only to senses animated by imagination, can nonetheless arrest the otherwise ceaseless play of metaphysical and genealogical phantasy.

When Hegel described the Gothic cathedral, he stressed that such architecture has the capacity to make stone—despite its heaviness—appear to ascend. Yet it is as if the builders of the great cathedrals at Strasbourg,

Cologne, and Chartres only learned to carry out by art what nature had always been capable of bringing about in shaping the mountains. For all their stony massiveness, especially where, above the tree line, they become sheer stone, the peaks are utterly ascensional, no less so than the face of a Gothic cathedral. The ascensional character of the peaks surrounding Soglio is enhanced by their sheer elevation, by the fact that they lie far above the town, far above most every observation point one can find even above the town. And in Sils Maria, as we observed, there are mountains that display their ascensional character even more graphically by way of various patterns of vertical striation. Up toward the peaks there are lines and arcs that point and sweep upward like the pillars of the great cathedrals, rendering the mountains still more ascensional by nature, gathering earth manifestly to sky.

13

Earthbound

Near Panzano
Toscana
18 July 1998

The earth is almost all that matters. It is upon the earth that we stand and move, even when we lift our eyes beyond the earth, toward the heaven. It is across the earth's expanses that we go to others; and these expanses we share with others or take from them or lose to them. It is across its fields and through its woods that we go in search of what life requires. Even our cities must be accommodated to the contours of the earth, and even there where agrarian economy is displaced by another, there remains at least a faint sense of the source beyond. It is in the earth that we plant and from the earth that we let things grow. Its bounty is our nourishment and our delight. Even the water that life requires is gathered by the earth. It is upon the earth, drawing support from it, that we build the shelters we need as protection from the elements and from the threat of other living things. What we use for building—stone, wood, or whatever—is taken, directly or indirectly, from the earth. We feast our eyes upon the beauty of the earth, above all when life upon it is vibrant and abundant and it offers to our senses its profusion of flowering and growth, but also even in the desolation of winter when hope and anticipation come to the aid of our senses and let us imagine the renewal to come.

Tuscan landscape

The earth is no mere object of our perception; it is not something merely to be seen, as we see things on the earth or even as we see one another. When we take it in this way, we have already become oblivious to the manifold and complex comportment to the earth that belongs to the proper bearing of humans and that continues to bind us to the earth even in our oblivion. If we go still further and construe the earth as a mere mass of matter, whether in the ancient or the modern sense of the term, then the oblivion will have doubled back upon itself and will have reached, it seems, its utter extreme.

There were vineyards in all directions as far as the rolling hills would allow us to see. We were in the heart of the Chianti country, and dedication to tending the vine was inscribed everywhere. This most cherished fruit has been cultivated here for centuries; and, even amidst the innovations that modern technology has introduced, guidance still comes largely from traditional knowledge concerning the soil, the vines, and the various vicissitudes of nature with which the vintner must deal. We could see that the lives not only of those in the countryside but also of the villagers were thoroughly engaged in tending and ensuring the exceptional bounty that the earth could produce in this region.

Most remarkably, the landscape had the appearance of pure nature. To be sure, signs of human presence and intervention were everywhere: there were the highly cultivated vineyards as well as small villages and individual houses scattered across the landscape. Yet all these were set so perfectly into the landscape that they seemed to belong there almost by nature. Only the slightest fancy was needed in order to regard them as having sprung from the earth, requiring—like the grapes—only the help of sun and rain and perhaps a bit of guidance by skilled human hands. Inhabited and tended for so many centuries, the landscape appeared to be adapted to our needs and purposes without relinquishing its natural character; it appeared as if it had adapted itself to these needs and purposes rather than being submitted to them by human intervention. It was this natural harmony that gave the landscape its distinctive beauty. It was a beauty that, while thoroughly natural, attested at the same time to the way in which humans belonged to the landscape.

A friend who lived in this region had arranged for us to stay in a stone house near the old farmhouse where he lived. It was impossible to tell whether the house was relatively new or whether it had stood there for centuries and had been only recently remodeled. Like other houses, like the landscape itself, it had a certain timelessness about it; or rather, it seemed to take part only in the time of nature, that of the seasons and of the day. Yet, most remarkably, there were almost no windows in the house; as in the old farmhouse where we had dined with our friend, there were only a couple of tiny panes up almost to the ceiling, admitting a

Stone house in Tuscany

little light but offering little view of the surroundings. It is of course difficult to build large windows in a stone house constructed by traditional methods. Yet it was as if the house were designed to offer respite from the incomparable beauty of the landscape, preparing us to respond all the more joyously when, the following morning, we stepped out into the light.

14
Silence

Järvenpää
near Helsinki
8 June 2002

Music has only the most indifferent relation to place. While music must be performed somewhere, it can in principle be performed in any place where competent musicians are assembled. Furthermore, it is for the most part indifferent to the place where it is performed; except in a few cases such as Gabrieli's *Canzoni,* music is not composed to be performed at any particular place; and unless external conditions impede the performance, it is largely unaffected by the place of its performance. The acoustics and thus the reception will be better in some places than in others, but the performance as such is relatively independent of these topical factors. In its indifference to place, the musical work stands in marked contrast to the architectural edifice, which not only is erected at a particular, appropriate place but also is itself fitted to, built into, that place.

Yet if distinct from architecture in this respect, music is in another respect akin to architecture: like architecture, music is nonrepresentational, at least in the case of so-called pure or absolute music, that is, music that is neither dramatic (as in opera) nor programmatic. Music is not at all mimetic in character; it does not imitate anything. Its sense does not lie in the production of an image of something, as a painting, for instance, may be taken as an image of a real or imaginary landscape or as a sculpture may provide an image of the imaginary figure of a god. Thus, in particular, music does not represent a place; it is not linked to place by a representational function, and so in this sense too it is indifferent to place. In this regard music would seem to be even more indifferent to place than is poetry: for whereas epic, dramatic, and even lyric poetry (as well as their modern developments in the novel and the short story) often are such as to bring forth an inner image of a certain real or imaginary place with more or less determinateness, pure music produces no representation of any place. While one may grant that music can evoke a certain abstract spatiality and movement, that music is thus by no means purely temporal, it has no link to any singular place, not even one that is purely imaginary. One may indeed characterize Sibelius' *Seventh Symphony* by means of the metaphor of glacial movement, but only if, in deploying the metaphor, one lifts it above everything topical and singular.

And yet, as the work of a composer, music has a place of origin. To be sure, music is detached from its place of origin: this place is not a privileged site for performance of the music composed there, is perhaps not even a suitable site for performance; and most assuredly music does not reflect its origin, does not produce an image of its place of origin. Yet if music is thus detached from its topical origin, the converse does not hold: to one who visits the place of origin, this place is not indifferent to having been the site of composition, especially if it has been preserved as in Salzburg, Tribschen, and Järvenpää.

I had been in Helsinki for a week lecturing on art, specifically on the question of the origin of the artwork. Though the context was one in which the sense of origin was shifted quite beyond the ordinary sense, precisely what was interrogated was the relation of art to the opening and establishing of place in an originary sense. Partly for this reason, only scant consideration was given to actual artworks (and then only by appeal to memory) and almost none at all to the singular places in which artworks are created.

It was only a short drive north from Helsinki to Järvenpää. Here in 1904 Sibelius built his house Ainola, which became his permanent residence and which now is preserved as a museum. The house is situated on a wooded slope that offers a spacious view over the fields to nearby Lake Tuusulanjärvi. Even before Sibelius settled there, other Finnish artists such as the painter Pekka Halonen had already taken up residence in the region. Sibelius' move to Järvenpää, following the completion of his first two symphonies, marked a turning point in his creative work. The relative simplicity and restraint of the *Third Symphony*, composed in Järvenpää, are indicative of this turn.

Sibelius moved to Järvenpää in search of the tranquility he needed in order to compose. His desire was to escape from the noise and distractions of Helsinki. What he sought, above all, in the idyllic setting in Järvenpää was silence.

The move to Järvenpää was also motivated by the composer's intense relationship with nature and his desire to work in a setting where he would be surrounded by nature. His keen attachment to nature is attested by the reports given by Santeri Levas, who served as Sibelius' private secretary for the last twenty years of the composer's life. Levas reports, for instance, that Sibelius often spoke of how intensely he had been affected by simple natural things or occurrences, especially during his childhood. Reportedly, Sibelius once declared: "Then I lived in nature. Even today I remember some dense grass that grew high above my head, and how I felt that I was within the grass and that I had entirely grown up with it." Levas relates also that Sibelius often carried with him a matchbox filled with moss, because through the scent of the moss he found it possible to transport himself into the atmosphere of a secluded woods. Levas tells also of a warm summer evening when he and Sibelius were strolling in the garden and the composer, evidently enjoying the sublime silence of nature, suddenly said: "A summer evening like this banishes all cares. In the presence of nature I always feel a sense of liberation."

There is perhaps no saying how Sibelius' profound attachment to nature figures in his music, though perhaps some indication can be gleaned from a work such as his *Hymn to the Earth,* a cantata for mixed chorus and orchestra, in which he set to music the words of the Finnish poet Eino Leino. The poet's words already border on song, and it is as if Sibelius' music releases and completes what is already under way in the poetry. The cantata, sung in the original Finnish, concludes with a strophe that may be translated as follows:

> The valleys join our song,
> the broad meadows join our song,
> the wide pastures join our song,
> the cattle bells join our song,
> the shores of heaven resound,
> the trumpets of the shores resound,
> they resound with the festival of light;
> Earth, sacred, Earth!
> Earth, sacred, generous, prodigal with gifts.
> Earth, sacred, Earth!

Levas reports that Sibelius himself sometimes drew connections between his music and natural occurrences, connections that often were magical, fantastical: for instance, that just as he put his pen to the score of the *Fifth Symphony* for the last time, twelve white swans landed on the lake, swam in a broad circle three times around, and then flew away.

In Järvenpää, Sibelius worked in the silence of the natural surroundings. This silence is, in a sense, transposed into his music. There is perhaps no composer who has been more skillful and effective in inscribing silence in the midst of music, as integral to the music itself. Perhaps most impressive in this regard is the integration of silence in the final moments of the *Fifth Symphony:* after the brilliant, soaring finale to the last movement, there is an abrupt interval of silence, followed then by a series of four subtly different chords separated by unusually long intervals of silence, and then, after another interval of silence, the resolution brought by the final two chords. It is as if in each of these silences the entire finale—perhaps this entire festive symphony—is repeated, silently reiterated, gathered into its ending.

Sibelius' silences were always related to his music; yet, beyond a point, the silence came to replace rather than enhance the music. In 1924 he completed his *Seventh Symphony,* which initially—and significantly—was called *Fantasia sinfonica.* This symphony differs from the other six in that

Final page of the score of Sibelius' *Fifth Symphony*

it was written without division into movements; this feature is indicative of the rigorous form that Sibelius achieved in this utterly incomparable work. It is a form that seems to have liberated the most profound musical resources, to have set free the most inevitable movement of tonalities. That this freedom and what is released through it exceed the possibility of verbal expression is attested by one of Sibelius' critical admirers, Olin Downes: "There are no words to describe this freedom, this powerful unity, this absolute consistency, this irresistible mastery."

Only two years later, in 1926, Sibelius wrote his last major work, the tone poem *Tapiola*. Thereafter, except for some very minor pieces for violin and piano composed in 1929, he wrote—that is, published—nothing else. When he died in 1957 at the age of ninety-two, he had remained silent for nearly thirty years. Yet while persisting in this silence, publishing nothing, Sibelius nonetheless insisted—according to Levas' testimony—that he continued to compose. At one point he is reported to have said to his secretary: "I have many sketches for my *Eighth Symphony*." Though later, in 1945, he told Levas that he had destroyed the whole work, that he had "put it in the fire," Levas reports that as late as 1953 Sibelius still insisted that he was working on a new symphony. As his silence continued, rumors and expectations of a new symphony grew. So strong were the expectations that major orchestras secured the rights to premier the new symphony. But the silence remained unbroken, and even after his death the new symphony was not to be found among his papers. To the end and beyond, Sibelius remained—painfully, no doubt—silent.

We drove directly to Järvenpää and parked a short walk away from Ainola. Strolling through the beautifully wooded surroundings, we stopped at the grave site and stood silently for several minutes. In the house everything had been preserved as it was before the death of Sibelius' wife Aino in 1969. Everything one would expect was there: a large studio room with Sibelius' piano in the corner, his library with long rows of books still on the shelves, and, at one end, a sitting area where he would presumably have received friends; his desk and chair were also there and looked indeed as though he might have been seated there composing a new symphony only a short time ago. Now, decades after his death, everything was there except the music. Yet everything that was there suggested the music, evoked the music. The place had the form of surroundings in which only the center, to which everything else is oriented, remained absent—or rather, as the silent sounding of music, engaged an unspeakable exchange between presence and absence. There, in that evocative place, the music sounded silently. It was not just as if one heard the powerful tonalities of the *Seventh Symphony,* not just a matter of pretending or emptily imagining. There, in that place, one heard those tonalities, heard them in perhaps the same way that the composer himself would have heard them before they ever sounded, as he was composing. There, in that place, one heard the great symphony silently, heard it sounding in silence.

15

Storm at Dusk

Münstertal
Baden
19 June 2002

They were the longest days of the year. They were the days when the sun's path is longest, the path on which, as always, it measures out time itself with a visibility binding on all. While providing the measure of time, this most prominent and most public of natural clocks has its own time extended to the extreme; it lingers in its metrodoric visibility, continuing to shine well beyond the time when in other seasons night would have fallen. In the far north the almost unlimited extension of the day into the white night profoundly alters the sense of time. But even here in southwest Germany the extending of the day broaches another remarkable phenomenon: as the day lengthens, the transition from day to night is also extended, so that twilight lingers for an inordinately long time. At dusk it seems as if time were stretched, as if the interval in which day becomes night—the time of dusk—were so extended that the transition became imperceptible and time seemed to stand still. It is as if these longest of days brought, at their limit, a kind of suspension of time in time. It is as if each of these days were bounded by a bit of timelessness, as if they referred, ever so discreetly, to eternity, though to an eternity belonging to time rather than set over against it.

This year these longest of days brought heat far in excess of what is to be expected in such temperate regions. The sky remained absolutely cloudless, and the only change perceptible in it was that brought about by the haze, which accumulated as the hot days continued. Under these conditions the lengthening of the day had the effect of extending the hours of sunshine; meanwhile the short night brought less relief from the heat built up during the long day. The steady intensification during the day was such that even the approach of evening had little effect; even during the extended dusk the intense heat remained almost unabated. Throughout the long day and into the evening, listlessness prevailed, even among those who, impelled by necessity—by a necessity linked to time and nature—persevered in their agrarian labor. Only the children seemed somewhat immune, at least those whose shouts of joy could be heard as they doused themselves in the stream that ran through the valley.

It was after days of such heat that, one evening as dusk had just set in, the thunderstorm finally came. The clouds gathered in the east, over the highest mountains. The approach of the storm first became visible as the sky grew dark there over the mountains. At the same time, its approach was sounded by the distant rumblings of thunder, echoing in the mountains. The clouds spread rapidly over the valley, their canopy casting its darkness over the entire scene, which appeared even more somber as the brightness of the day persisted in memory. As the storm came nearer, the hot, heavy air was penetrated ever more frequently by cool, moist drafts, refreshing beyond measure. Then, the pace ever quickening, nature in its elemental force brought the downpour of hail and rain, giving voice to it as it pounded the fields and meadows and the roofs of the sturdy houses. Whatever was unsheltered was quickly and thoroughly drenched, and all around one sensed the coolness amidst the fury of the elements.

During the approach of the storm, the farmer in whose house we were staying had busily gone about sheltering as many things as possible from its force, securing whatever was fitted out to be secured and covering the tender young growth in the vegetable garden. Once the storm arrived and the driving rain compelled him to retreat indoors, he appeared at the door of our apartment, his face expressing a curious blend of wonder and recognition as he gestured toward the storm raging outside. He uttered a single word: *Natur*—and then disappeared. Other living things, too, acknowledged in their own way the force of nature and the need to take shelter from it. Across the meadow the cows were huddled under the trees at the edge of the woods.

As dusk stretched on, the storm passed over, moving westward, out onto the plain, leaving behind in the valley air so refreshingly cool that already the memory of the intensely hot days began to pale. In the west, thunder continued to rumble. Out on the plain the strange somber glow of the storm clouds blended with the afterglow of sunset, producing a radiance that, while hardly even suggestive of any colors other than gray, was nonetheless manifestly too brilliant to be called simply gray. Though the sun had long since set, the radiant sky still held the last trace of sunlight; and it continued, if less and less frequently, to be streaked with brilliant flashes of lightning. By the time the storm had passed completely out of sight, the long solstitial dusk had given way to night.

When everything is covered by darkness and little is offered to vision other than the starry heaven, memory and reflection come more actively into play, living memory of what has passed and thoughtful reflection that situates it within multiple configurations of sense. Thus the force and display of the elemental that had been witnessed could be set over against the variety of human concerns, reducing those concerns to their proper scope. Before such a configuration it can come to light that there are different ways of giving things their due, that there are various measures by which to do justice to humans, to things, and to the elements. As the storm can be given its due by letting it rage, by letting the raging confluence of elements be manifest, as, sheltered from it, one is drawn into astonishment and wonder at nature's marvelous spectacle.

16

Solstitial Fires

Vallée de Saint-Amarin
Alsace
21 June 2003

The conclusion is astonishing yet compelling: there is no such thing as fire. The exclusion is decisive: among the things that are, the word has no proper reference; there is nothing that as such would exemplify what the word means, no instance corresponding in fact to what the word signifies. Though fire appears to exist, indeed not just to exist but to burn, to glow, to flame, to give off heat and smoke, to penetrate and consume things, the appearance is mere appearance, nothing but appearance. To be sure, the red glow, the yellow flames, all those phenomena that are readily identified as fire persist in appearing; they continue to be vividly present to the senses even after the conclusion has been firmly established that there is no such thing as fire. They are appearances that dazzle even the most perceptive observer, shinings that bewilder and bedevil the senses, natural illusions that can no more be dispelled than can the appearance that the sun sets.

Yet however persistent the appearance of fire may be, however persistently fire appears to exist, however convincingly its appearance seems to be that of something existent, there is no such thing as fire. This is the present-day view, not just an opinion held here and there, not just a theory defended by a certain party, but a view certified by modern research, a result established by rigorous procedures and hence universally binding, a conclusion requiring universal consent. It is remarkable nonetheless that fire has disappeared, that it has vanished from the sight of modern research—remarkable not only because of the persistence and vividness with which it continues to appear to exist, even to the most inveterate practitioner of modern research, but also because of the bond that intimately connects visible appearance—and disappearance—with fire. Though advanced technology provides means for attenuating the connection, even to the point of sheer metaphorization, fire is otherwise the source of light; and without light nothing becomes visible, nothing visible appears. Without the appearance of fire, without the glow and the flames that attest to its existence, there would be no visible appearance at all, no visibility as such. All visible appearance—so it appears—relies finally on this deceptive appearance, on this natural illusion that is readily taken to attest that there is such a thing as fire.

The banishment of fire from the view of modern research contrasts sharply with the significance attached to it by the ancients. According to the classical Greek philosophers, fire not only is one of the four elements but also, of the four, is the one that is most mobile and that can most sharply and thoroughly penetrate the other elements. Yet, of these elements, fire is the only one that modern research has dispelled, though, assuredly, the others have been deprived of their status as elements, reduced to mere compounds, mixtures, or mixtures of compounds. Still, no modern researcher will dispute whether water, air, or earth exists. Only fire has been banished. Only fire has completely vanished from view. The present-day view makes it indisputable: fire does not exist as such. What once appeared to be fire—and still deceptively appears as such—is, instead, merely a chemical process, rapid oxidation, which happens to give off heat and light. The flames that appear to dance before one's eyes are nothing but this discharge, certainly no existing thing or element, virtually nothing at all. Almost the same can be said of the great fire of the heaven: modern research has established that the solar fire—that is, what appears to be solar fire—is also a process, indeed a process that as such is even more insistently invisible than that of ordinary combustion, though, as an atomic, rather than merely chemical, process, nuclear fusion gives off an enormously greater abundance of heat and light than do ordinary chemical processes. These processes occur at the limit of visibility, at a limit that involves intrinsic resistance to being rendered visible. Yet these virtually invisible processes constitute the primary source of visibility as such. They are processes withdrawn from the very visibility they make possible. Fire—even the intense glow of the solstitial sun, even the leaping, towering flames of a gigantic bonfire—is no more than a deceptive appearance that crops up on the way from the invisible source to visibility as such.

Who would—in light of this firmly established view—still be concerned with fire, not just with its effects, not just with utilization of or protection from its effects, but with fire itself as it appears before the senses? Who would still be attentive to the radiance of the midsummer sun or to the flames that soar heavenward as if akin to that radiance?

In a remote valley in southwest Alsace, a festival is celebrated each year at the time of the summer solstice. At this time of year the sun climbs so high on its path across the sky that the day is extended to maximal length. If these longest days of the year happen also to be relatively cloudless, there is sunshine for more than sixteen hours. Since, in addition, the periods of twilight are also protracted, night shrinks to a mere five hours or less. These are, then, the days when things are most exposed to the intense summer sun. They are the days when everything is polarized toward the raging fire of heaven. They are also, proverbially, the days of midsummer madness, when the extension of day and the shrinkage of night, together with the intense heat of the blazing sun, all conspire to drive humans to distraction.

Such festivals as that celebrated in the Vallée de Saint-Amarin go back to prehistory. With the advent of the Church these ancient rites, though tolerated rather than abolished, underwent a transformation. The transformation consisted in a change of significance, of what the festival was taken to signify, to celebrate. Upon the pagan celebration of this time of natural disequilibrium, there was superimposed a religious significance: the festival was dedicated to John the Baptist, was transformed into a celebration of his nativity. The only connection that remained with the natural phenomena proper to this time of seemingly perpetual sunlight was extremely remote: as the precursor of Christ, John the Baptist is biblically represented as proclaiming that while he baptizes with water, the one who will come after him will baptize with fire. Even still today the Alsatians call the festival *Feux de la Saint-Jean.*

But except for the name, little remains of the overlay with which the Church sought to tame the celebration of the fire of summer. The festival is held all along the valley at various sites atop the mountains that tower above the valley where the villages lie. Each village has its own celebration on the heights just above. People began gathering long before dusk, thronging into the clearing that was to serve for the festival, each seeking out an optimal vantage point from which—hours later, when night had finally banished the blazing sun of the solstitial day—to witness the spectacle and experience with boundless joy the raging fire.

Everything had been painstakingly prepared. At the particular site where, almost by chance, we settled in to watch—and indeed to take part in—the celebration, there were three large wooden towers that had been carefully constructed. The entire site was organized around these large structures, which were broad at the base and tapered almost to a point at the top. In Alsatian dialectic such a tower is called a *Fackel,* that is, a torch. Two of the towers were the same size, but the third, which stood between them, was much larger. They were constructed using long shafts formed from saplings or even somewhat larger trees; the bark had been removed, and the bare shafts had been cut to the proper length and carefully notched so as to fit tightly together. Thus the structures were quite well built, and despite their enormous size they were very stable. The largest tower was three to four meters across at the base and some twenty meters high. Inside the almost pyramidal frame formed by the notched, vertically positioned shafts, there appeared to be a great deal of brush, consisting primarily of twigs and smaller limbs presumably trimmed from the saplings used to make the shafts. According to one written account the entire structure was erected around a central fir; most likely the structures had at some time been constructed in this manner, but it was impossible to discern whether this was still the case. At the very

Wooden towers above Vallée de Saint-Amarín

top of the tower there stood a small evergreen; it could have been the very tip of a central fir protruding from the top of the tower; but its appearance was more like that of a small tree set atop the tower, an arborescent sacrifice to be consumed at the moment when finally the flames soared to the top of the tower and engulfed the entire structure.

It was quite some time before, as dusk came on, the first of the two smaller towers was lit. By this time a certain intoxication had taken hold of the crowd as more and more people arrived, milling around or seeking out a good vantage point. Already there was loud music, its resounding making it a bit raucous, and exuberant dancing on a low platform set up near the middle of the site. There was also the smoky scent of pork and lamb roasted over open fires, and people were downing the charred meat with quantities of local red wine. The atmosphere was one of self-abandonment to the joy of these hours when, as the blazing sun sank below the horizon, humans would themselves venture to ignite their own fires of heaven. Always, ever since Prometheus stole fire from the gods and gave it to mortals, the difference has proven so slight as to be almost imperceptible, undecidable, the difference between offering tribute and sacrifice to what animates the heaven and challenging—even if only with a symbolic replica—its supremacy and authority.

At first, once the tower had been lit, the brush, which caught fire immediately, emitted a great deal of smoke. For a time the smoke hovered around the base of the tower, but then as the upward draft took hold, it billowed heavenward like a whirlwind, its motion bringing to mind such words as *Wirbel, Wirbelwind, Wirbelsturm.* Finally the flames leaped up, as if to overtake the dense smoke and drive it still more forcefully into the darkening sky. The mountains echoed with the clamor of the spectators, which rose to its highest pitch and intensity at the moment when the flames suddenly engulfed the entire structure.

As the long dusk continued, the flames gradually consumed the tower. It was remarkable how long this required despite the huge, raging fire. The structures were so well built, their joints so tightly set, that they continued to stand even after much of the material of which they consisted had gone up in smoke. Indeed we were uncertain which was more remarkable, the capacity of the well-built structure to endure the raging fire for so long before finally toppling or the consuming power of the flames to which even such a strong, stable structure finally succumbed.

As dusk moved toward night, the second of the smaller towers was lit with brands taken from the first. In the diminished daylight the flames seemed still more intense, and as they engulfed the entire tower and consumed the small tree set atop it, the aura of sacrifice was enhanced. Only after night had fallen and the charred skeleton of the second tower had begun to collapse was a brand taken from it and used to ignite the gigantic tower that stood, still pristine, between the blackened remains of the other

Wooden tower aflame

two. An unearthly cry went up from the crowd as the tower was lit and once more, in tones still more shrill, as the flames leaped up to engulf the giant structure. A tremor of excitement, the spell of rapture, swept over the crowd as the flames soared beyond the top of the tower, up into the heaven, lighting up the nocturnal sky.

Yet it was and remained—even if for only a few hours—a nocturnal sky, lit by the solstitial fires, to be sure, but still nocturnal. However high these fires may have soared above the mountains, they provided only a remote image of the fire of heaven. For the sun is quite otherwise; it is aloof from humanity, and, unlike terrestrial fire, unlike even the fires that raged above the Alsatian valley as the longest day of the year came to an end, the solar fire is utterly withdrawn from human instigation, control, or interference. On the other hand, its effect is linked by bonds of necessity to the very possibility of human life.

It is not surprising, then, that at least since the time of Egyptian ascendancy the sun has often been represented as the king and the king as the sun. Without the sun there could be no human life; to live is—in the Homeric phrase—to see the light of the sun. Its destructiveness is of the same order, its power to scorch the earth until living things wither away. If the sun is a natural image of virtually unlimited power, then there is reason to wonder whether the bond between fire and power can ever be completely broken. Any but the most rudimentary genealogy would seem to reveal a complicity between the enforcement of power and the forging of metals, for which fire is requisite. Can the will to power be thought concretely—in its somatic and material deployment and not just as the essence of subjectivity—without reference to fire?

Among the early Greek philosophers there was one for whom fire became a universal theme. Heraclitus of Ephesus regarded fire not just as one among several elements but rather as that through the conception of which one could think the universe itself, which he called—using the word in a sense that was just becoming current—the cosmos. By thinking fire, it is—according to Heraclitus—possible to think the cosmos because—in a sense of the word that the Greek philosophers first rigorously determined—the cosmos *is* fire.

With the words taken over from Preclassical antiquity, translation is always perilous, not only because of their removal in time but also because of the difficulty of gauging the impact of philosophical thought upon the inherited language. Though *cosmos* gradually came to be identified with the universe (the all, the whole to which all things belong), it retained, even long after Heraclitus, a hint of its old sense, that of an ordered array like that of the starry heaven. The word translated as *fire* is perhaps even more remote from what today is understood by fire, especially if fire is understood as something that does not as such exist, as a mere deceptive appearance accompanying certain invisible processes. For the ancients, on the contrary, fire is preeminently the source of visibility. It is that which, itself visible as such, lets all things become visible.

Translating the fragmentary passages still extant from Heraclitus' writings is still more perilous, for these passages are handed down as citations in the texts of later authors, who wrote with very different purposes in mind and from orientations quite divergent from any that Heraclitus could be supposed to have taken. Some of the authors from whom the passages are taken lived nearly a millennium after Heraclitus. Nonetheless, even in an appropriately minimalist translation, many of the fragments succeed in making something manifest. Consider, for instance, such a translation of the passage numbered as Fragment 30, which derives from Clement of Alexandria, a convert to Christianity who lived in the second and third centuries A.D. and who was renowned for the comparisons he drew between so-called paganism and Christianity. As cited by Clement, the passage, minimally translated, reads: "This cosmos was not made either by gods or by humans, but it always was and is and will be: ever-living fire, kindling measures and extinguishing measures." In saying that the cosmos (all things in their visible array) is—and always was and will be—fire, Heraclitus is not putting forth the thesis that everything is made of fire, as, for instance, all swords are made of metal. On the contrary, the cosmos is not made at all, neither by gods nor by humans. Heraclitus simply does not conceive the cosmos according to the model of something made; thus he cannot be said to have regarded the cosmos as composed of fire as a primary material. Most certainly he does not regard fire as the matter of which the cosmos consists; indeed prior to Aristotle there is no concept of matter in Greek thought—not, however, because these early philosophers failed to come up with such a concept but rather because they thought the cosmos otherwise than in terms of making. Above all, Heraclitus thought the visible array of all things by attaching that array to the source of its visibility, a source itself visible and thus called ever-living.

It is in this sense—in this sense of the *is*—that the cosmos is fire. And it is in this sense that another passage, a confirmatory one, is to be read, the passage numbered as Fragment 90 and handed down by Plutarch. In minimal translation, the passage reads: "There is exchange of all things for fire and of fire for all things, as of goods for gold and of gold for goods."

Even toward the end of antiquity, several centuries later, after enormous transformations, the sense of the cosmic uniqueness of fire still persists. Plotinus declares that fire is more beautiful than any other bodies, because it has the rank of form (*eidos*) in relation to the other elements. Its place is above all the other elements, and it is so fine that it is close to the incorporeal. Plotinus observes, most remarkably, that all other things take their color—that is, their visible appearance as such—from fire, and in this sense fire shines and glistens, he says, as if it were eidetic. All other things become faint and dull without the light of fire.

Here, then, at the heart of what will be called Neoplatonism, the earlier Greek sense of fire lives on. For at the heart of Platonism there is the thought of the eidetic as that which makes things visible, as that which shines through things in such a way as to let things come to light as they are. Among the elements only fire has this capacity, and for this reason—because of its shining and glistening—it is akin to the eidetic, indeed as close to being eidetic as any element can be.

This eidetic elemental is what was celebrated there above the Alsatian villages on the first night of summer. This elemental fire is what was greeted there with joy and self-abandonment as it lit up the night sky in simulation of the source of all visibility.

17

Ancient Memories

Athens/Delphi
10–11 July 2003

It shone quite apart, as if, being there, it belonged also apart. Finally evening had come, bringing relief from the blistering heat, almost unendurable amidst the fumes from the traffic and the thermal reflections from the surfaces of the streets and buildings. Even what sanctuaries there are in modern-day Athens—shaded areas, even parks—were so overheated by these effects that they offered little escape. But as the sun set and night came on, the heat became less intense. We sat in an outdoor restaurant just across from the Acropolis, indeed just opposite the Parthenon. It was illuminated, and, as we looked up and across at it, it looked almost surreal, this most familiar of Greek temples, pictured everywhere, even replicated in an American city, but now seen perched above Athens and artificially illuminated, almost as it might have been painted by Magritte. The sight would have seemed less odd had the temple been illuminated simply by moonlight. Yet the odd effect had a peculiar appropriateness, for the artificial lighting intensified the impression already created by the temple's elevation above the hustle and bustle of the city: it appeared as if it belonged to an entirely different order, as if its presence were a presence of an entirely different sort from that of the things below in the city. It shone forth as if untouched, even untouchable, by all that was going on beneath it, as if its very existence belonged to a higher plane, as if, being there, it belonged also apart.

This appearance, though intensified by the conditions, was no doubt linked to all that was evoked by memory of what the temple once was, the abode of the goddess who oversaw the incomparable beginnings achieved in the ancient city. Even if now it shone differently—in modern lighting, in ruins, with the goddess conspicuously absent—it appeared nonetheless apart from the mundane human preoccupations, no less so than was the goddess herself.

The following morning we set out for Delphi. It was not my first visit to Delphi. I had been there more than twenty-five years earlier on my first trip to Greece. Walking up the Sacred Way past the various treasuries, then through the area where Apollo was said to have slain the Python and thus to have acquired the sanctuary as his own, on up to the ruins of the great temple, and finally to the theatre and the stadium, I had sought some sense of how Apollo and all that we know was connected with him—order, measure, but also dream, phantasy, art—belonged to this utterly wild, remote, yet beautiful site. The tension was also expressed in the association that this abode of Apollo had also with Dionysus: the ancients attest that in winter what was sung in Delphi was the dithyramb to Dionysus and not the Paean of Apollo, also that during this season the Maenads held their wild dances on the snow-covered slopes of Mt. Parnassos.

Returning to this sacred place so many years later brought an incomparable fulfillment of memory. It was perhaps only on this second visit that I could realize how deeply impressive the place had been on the first visit. For only what impresses deeply remains so abiding in memory. As I walked up the Sacred Way, it was perfect repetition, not an occurrence as if for the first time, but rather the rare event of experiencing a site again with the same intensity as at first. No doubt this experience was to a large extent due to the fact that in such a place memory does not occur simply as one's own. It has little or nothing to do with acts of remembering that would, as it were, retrieve something held within; rather, it comes from without, is evoked by the place, and occurs in response to this evocation. Here the place itself bore and made visibly manifest the memory of the

Delphi

Greek beginning. That it was deeply impressive resulted from the fact that the traces of this beginning were deeply impressed on the site itself.

A tension not unlike that embodied in its gods was displayed by the site, much more faintly, no doubt, than in antiquity but nonetheless evident even in the ruins. The site was such as to yoke together expansiveness and concentration, to hold these together in their tension: expansiveness up to the heights of Mt. Parnassos and out across the valley all the way to the Bay of Corinth in the distance; concentration in the various edifices that remain, even though in ruins, and most powerfully in the remaining columns and other ruins of the temple of Apollo.

18

Chora

Naxos

12–13 July 2003

The main town, located on the western side of the island, has the same name as the island itself. Yet it is called not only Naxos but also Chora. Recalling how decisive the name *chora* was for ancient thought, that in it was concentrated a thinking of place—of what later came to be called place—so originary that it disrupted, in advance, the basic schema of virtually all subsequent thought, our arriving at a place so named could not go unremarked. Nor could the location of our hotel, three kilometers south of the town, just outside Chora. For, as a Platonic locution, *chora* names—without being quite sustainable as a name—that which enables all being outside, all exteriority. Even the still unformed elements—fire, air, water, and earth, while they are still not quite themselves—have their expanse only through the spacing of the chora.

Long before we arrived, almost as soon as we caught our first glimpse of the island, we could see the magnificent square arch that now serves as a gateway to Naxos. It is all that remains of a temple of Apollo, begun in the sixth century B.C. but never finished. The arch stands on the islet of Palatia, which is joined to the main town by a causeway. I remembered that on a brief visit to Naxos a few years earlier, I had walked out to the arch in the midday heat, absorbed by the site and by the sound of the

Gateway to Naxos

waves, becoming almost oblivious to the town and to everything else except the arch, which stands there in its utter solitude upon the small, almost bare islet. Again, as we now approached the harbor, I was struck by the way the arch stands there entirely alone, a gate opening onto the space of the town and of the island.

As we arrived, we could not but recall the ancient stories: how Ariadne, out of love, had come to Theseus' aid in defeating the Minotaur, how she had then sailed from Crete with her lover, only to be abandoned by him on Naxos, and how then eventually she was rescued by Dionysus. The story has lived on in various guises. Through the story as it has lived on, a *mythos* and a history are woven into the natural landscape of the island.

The story lived on among the ancients and lives on still in our time. In Athens it lived on in the ritual of sending an embassy to Delos each year, indeed in a vessel that was said to be the same as that in which Theseus had once sailed on his legendary voyage to Crete. The Athenians were said to have made a vow to Apollo at that time that if Theseus and his companions were saved, such an expedition would thereafter be dispatched annually. The story lived on also within another story, that of Socrates' death, which, according to the *Phaedo,* was delayed nearly a month because the expedition to Delos had sailed the day before Socrates' trial, and no executions were permitted while it was under way. In the *Phaedo* the story lived on also in that the dialogue conspicuously imitates Theseus' voyage: the nine Athenians and five foreigners who are named as being present at the scene of Socrates' death correspond to the nine young men and five maidens who accompanied Theseus on his voyage. Further correspondences abound, Socrates playing the role of Theseus, and death or the fear of death corresponding to the Minotaur. The most decisive turn in the dialogue is that in which Socrates enunciates and enacts what he himself calls a second sailing. In our time the story lives on in various guises, but none more remarkable than in Richard Strauss' opera *Ariadne on Naxos.* In the opera the story of Ariadne's abandonment by Theseus and ultimate rescue by Bacchus is preceded by a Prologue in *opera buffa* style; its setting is backstage as preparations are being made for the *opera seria* about Ariadne on Naxos, and it includes among its characters the fictive composer of the opera that is about to be performed. Even after the *opera seria* begins, the characters from the Prologue continue to intervene, the comedians trying, for instance, to cheer up the forsaken Ariadne with a song and a dance. Once Bacchus appears and both he and Ariadne are overpowered by the mystery of love, Ariadne's longing for death is transformed into a readiness to yield to love, and Bacchus becomes aware of his divinity for the first time. Then the characters of the *opera buffa* all withdraw, and the opera—as well as the opera within the opera—concludes with Ariadne and Bacchus celebrating in song their transfiguring love.

On the island of Naxos nature is indeed extraordinary. Though it required a few hours' repose, I soon began to sense again the elemental rhythm of the waves, which, because of the relatively high wind, came crashing against the shore. Walking in the town toward evening, we watched the intensely red, fiery ball sink behind the mountains of the neighboring island of Paros, the fire of heaven received by the earth.

Temple of Demeter, near Sangri, Naxos

This display of the elements seen from Chora prepared us for the other elemental sights we would witness as we traversed the island.

Next morning we set out in a Jeep to cross the island from west to east. Our first stop was at the Temple of Demeter near the small town of Sangri. What we saw was not the temple itself, not even really its ruins. Long ago a small Byzantine chapel had been built on what remained of the ancient temple's foundations, but recently the chapel had been removed entirely, and taking into account both the remains of the foundation and what is known about the form of the original temple, archeologists have erected on the site a replica not of the temple, but rather of its ruins: several columns, some of them shorter as if broken off, some with partial entablatures, also a couple of walls, and the floor. The smoothness and color of the stone make it quite evident that these are not really the ruins of the original temple but rather new ruins, ruins restored.

Yet, however curious these ruins may have seemed, they did suffice to allow us to envisage the site itself, which proved most remarkable. The temple was set atop a low hill, from which point it gathered and concentrated the surrounding countryside. In the distance, completely encircling the site, were fairly high mountains. Within the space of this enclosure, what was especially marvelous was the constant sound of the cicadas and the glistening of the olive trees that were scattered here and there on the surrounding landscape. It was striking how integrally the sounding of the cicadas and the shining of the olive trees belonged to the landscape as a whole. Indeed it was as though, with their singing, the cicadas provided the measure of the heat, of the midday sun's intensity. Meanwhile the olive trees, shining forth in the intense light, appeared to have taken their shape from the wind, seemed to have been blown by it so incessantly that they had assumed a shape corresponding to it; thus they served to give the measure of the wind, especially on days that, like today, were especially blustery.

We had a late lunch at a simple restaurant in Sangri, where, sitting under an arbor, we enjoyed the local cheese, local wine, and roasted lamb, all delicious. We managed minimal communication, though the proprietor spoke only Greek. Yet he was so hospitable that I could not resist trying a few words of Greek, which earned us a big smile and some ouzo to round out the meal. The few words I had uttered were not in any syntactic order, and the spaces between them would have had to be filled by lots of other words in order for the utterance to make proper sense. What was impressive was that his receptiveness, his hospitality, allowed him to understand despite the utterance's complete lack of syntactic and semantic spacings.

Precisely the same phenomenon, but in reverse and even more conspicuously, awaited us at our next stop, Chalki, a few kilometers to the northeast. Our destination was the distillery that produces kitro, a liqueur made from a lemon-like fruit and found only on Naxos. The man who showed us around and offered some tastings knew very little English. One of us tried German with him, and so subsequently he spoke German to her while to the rest of us he spoke English—or rather, he spoke what

Moutsouna Bay, Naxos

sounded like German and like English. When he first spoke to us, it seemed more or less understandable; at least we thought we had understood. But then we noticed the remarkable way in which he was constructing sentences in languages of which in fact he knew only a few words. In such a sentence there would be a couple of actual words—say, of English. But then the intervals before, after, and between these words he would fill in with sounds that sounded rather like English; and he would stamp a kind of seal on what he had said by means of gestures that suggested a certain obviousness or self-evidentness. Here, too, as when I had spoken with the restaurant proprietor, it was a matter of spacing. But now it all came from the side of the speaker, both the lack of proper spacings and the comportment that compensated for this lack, that by means of gestures and English-sounding sounds produced a compensatory spacing that made what he would say somewhat understandable. It seemed that on this island spacings were decisive everywhere, in the landscape, in the confluence of natural elements, and in speech.

From Chalki we headed up into the high mountains, passing through Filoti, which is built on the mountainside. Far above, perched on the very pinnacle of the highest peak, there was a small, white chapel, its location attesting to the elemental longing for heights. Continuing up the steep, winding road, we finally came to the summit, and then suddenly, spectacularly, there before us, far below, shone the sea on the eastern side of the island. Soon we came to the crossroads and turned off, descending precipitously on the very narrow and treacherous road that wound down to Moutsouna Bay and the fishing village of Moutsouna. The village and the bay are otherwise accessible only from the sea. We sat for a couple of hours in an outdoor taverna, enjoying the fresh bounty from the sea, marveling at the blueness and transparency of the water and at the purity and intensity of the light, as we looked out at other, smaller islands far in the distance. There is no more secluded site on Naxos and none where the perfection and beauty of the elements are more captivating and at the same time more reposeful.

19

Descent

Naxos
14 July 2003

This morning the high wind was gone. The sea around Chora had become calmer, and now the waves gently touched the shore, more like an embrace than an assault.

To someone who seldom observes the sea, the movement of the waves onto the shore may seem almost monotonous. But closer observation and proper attunement allow one to sense the endless variations of this theme, the constantly changing pattern of the sea's arrival on land. Only through such attunement to this communication between earth and sea was Debussy able to transform this phenomenon into a musical composition in which, without the artifice of mere imitation, one can hear not only the sound but also the sight of the sea.

We drove along the northwest coast of the island toward Apollonas. Though the mountains were not quite so high as those in the center of the island, the entire way was mountainous, the road narrow and winding.

Our first stop was at Kloster Faneromeni, dating from the seventeenth century. Perched just above the sea, it offered an open, expansive view out over the water into the distance. Yet everything about the Kloster indicated that the proper orientation was inward rather than outward. As we were admiring the altar, our attention was drawn to the space behind the altar,

Kouros just above Apollonas, Naxos

a space of reserve or withdrawal, which nonetheless disclosed itself as such through an opening in the altar. The contrast with the sheer ascendancy of the Gothic cathedral was striking: unlike an architecture that draws everything—even stone—upward, the architecture of the Kloster had an appropriateness to a divine who descends to the human, yet always with reserve, in withdrawal. How remarkable that this trace of antiquity remains.

As we continued, the road swung up onto the mountainside, though still running parallel to the coast. Far below, a series of lovely inlets and bays came into view, most of them showing no signs of human intervention or habitation. From the much higher and broader perspective afforded by the elevation of the road, we could see just how these little incursions of the sea serve to shape the coastline as a whole.

Finally we reached Apollonas and, leaving our car below in the town, walked up to the ancient marble quarry. On the edge of the quarry facing the town the *kouros* lay, almost horizontally. This colossus, sculpted in the seventh century B.C., was probably never considered finished; nor was it ever raised to an upright position. Yet, seeing it there on the mountain-side as the sun beat down and the cicadas chanted as if they would sing themselves to death, looking down at the lovely town and, beyond it, the sea, we could easily imagine what a sight it would have been: this Apollo of stone, more than ten meters high, standing in the slightly recessed space on the side of the mountain, overlooking his namesake town, tending it in the way proper to the god.

20

At Sea

Sailing between
Naxos and Delos
15 July 2003

Visiting Delos again was a practice of remembrance, of letting memories be evoked and perhaps intensified, memories of what had been experienced on our earlier visit to this utterly astonishing place, this expanse that, even in ruins, still appears sacred and prompts one to speak of the gods, to do so in another voice, in an almost foreign tone.

It is remarkable how perfectly the sanctuary on Delos is set into its site, how it is open, exposed, to the elements, to sea, wind, sun, and the rocky terrain. A more profound contrast with Christian sanctuaries could hardly be imagined. A sanctuary dedicated to a god who is proclaimed the one god, to a god abstracted from all the connections with nature that abound with the Greek gods, could never be so exposed to the elements and so set in its natural site. For the Greeks who built this sanctuary, nature was not a region of decline, of falling away from the divine, but rather was the very site of the appearance of the gods, the site into which the temples had to be built so as to receive the gods. Poseidon was god "of" the sea, not as a ruler aloof from the thalassic surface and depth and from all that shapes, illuminates, resists, and moves the sea, but rather precisely as belonging to the sea, as elementally bound up with it. His appearance was not to a self aloof from nature; instead, he appeared from the sea, in the sea, as the sea—or rather, he appeared in a manner that combines all three prepositional senses, that also exceeds them. Thus it was necessary that his temple be erected near the sea, that it be built into the surroundings of the sea. It could not have taken the form of a pure interior withdrawn from nature so as, through transcendence, to circumvent nature.

As, in the early morning, we had sailed from Naxos to Mikonos and then on a smaller ferry gone on to nearby Delos, the mood was one of quiet anticipation and also, for those of us visiting Delos for the second time, one of awakening remembrances. But after several hours of wandering among the ruins and opening our senses to the elemental site of the sanctuary, a very different attunement had come into play, and it remained determining throughout the trip back to Naxos.

As soon as we boarded the main ferry at Mikonos, I stationed myself outside at the rear corner of the deck. There were others on the deck, but most were sitting on long benches. Throughout the entire trip back to Naxos I stood silently looking out at the sea, feeling the wind and the sun, trying to sense to the utmost what was afforded by being at sea in such a place. I was quite aware that what could be sensed then and there would be elusive, that it could easily slip away from the words with which I would say it—even that it would necessarily exceed its expression, that the word *blue* would never quite be a match for the blueness of the Aegean.

The elements could not have been more manifestly in force, each as such and all in their elemental way of being together.

The sky was just as clear as it had been ever since our arrival on Naxos, that is, perfectly clear, no clouds whatsoever. Day after day it had remained the same, a purely recessive dome, an aithereal canopy, uncompromised by the shapes and movements of clouds. Pure cloudlessness is pure sky, admitting only sun, moon, and stars. It varies only as the light changes, the light that most properly belongs to it. Yet in such a sky the light hardly changes at all except at dawn and dusk. Throughout the rest of the day, it is as though the day were forever, as if it were the suspension of time itself. To be sure, the sun's position changes, and to this extent it

Sailing past small islands on the return to Naxos

marks time in the sky; but its shining does not change, and this uniformity casts a certain inconspicuousness over its movement, so that, while marking time, it also effaces the mark and to this extent marks time in the other sense of the phrase, that is, suspends time.

The earth is more purely visible, more visible as such, on the islands, perhaps most of all as one sails among the islands. The ferries often sail alongside tiny islands that are nothing but earth protruding from the sea without trees, virtually without vegetation. Yet more decisive than the simple lack of vegetation is the way in which what growing things there are belong to the earth. What predominates are forms of growth that have a peculiar affinity to the earth: thistles, brown grasses, olive trees.

View of Chora (Naxos)

Also, in mountains such as those on Naxos, in their very presence, earth and stone become most manifestly visible.

Sailing among the islands, one is constantly alert to the sea. Even on the islands it is seldom out of sight; even in the highest mountains on Naxos, one nearly always retains a view of the sea. Its presence is determined by the earth, by its belonging to the earth, by its being the earth's elemental opposite. The sea also welcomes and makes visible other elements, letting the sunlight shimmer on its surface, throwing up waves and perhaps whitecaps so as to announce the wind and make it visible.

Earth, sky, sun, sea, light, wind—sensed in their elusive presence—belong elementally together. Yet their confluences are so exorbitant that they violate what, since Greek antiquity itself, has been called logic. Here sense exceeds thought. This excess prescribes a fundamental reorientation.

Back on Naxos in the evening, we enjoyed a quiet dinner at our hotel. As soon as we arrived, the proprietor came to our table bringing what had become our preferred wine, a white called *Ariadne,* produced on Naxos.

Shortly thereafter he reappeared with a large tray of fish from which each of us selected the one desired. As he withdrew to grill our fish, we commented on how fresh the fish were. Within the last few hours no doubt they had been taken from the very sea on which we had been sailing and by which we had been so fascinated. The experience began to dawn on us there that evening, the experience of elemental immediacy; and it left us almost silent, as we listened to the gentle waves and looked up at the brilliant nocturnal sky.

21

Mountain Spectacle

Dobbiaco (Toblach)
Südtirol
22 July 2003

What do the mountains offer to a vision opened by imagination? What is it about the Alpine peaks that so entices sense, that enraptures vision while at the same time setting it in deep repose? How is it that these immobile stone masses at once energize vision to the utmost while bringing it to rest quietly in the spectacle, inhibiting the words that otherwise would initiate the labor of translation? How is it that so many are captivated immediately by the spectacle, as if transfixed before it? What evokes the intense, quiet, awestruck gaze? What is it that vision is drawn to apprehend in the look of such a spectacle?

It is not just the elevation that is evocative. The sky, too, is elevated, indeed in such a way as to determine the very sense of elevation; and yet the vision evoked by the sky is quite other than that called forth by the mountain spectacle. Whereas the sky offers pure elevation and unlimited recession, the mountains elevate something; or rather, they elevate an element that belongs to a completely different order of recession and that consequently, as such, ought not be elevated. What is distinctive about the mountains is that they elevate precisely that which otherwise provides the foundation for all things. They elevate that which underlies all things so absolutely that all founding and laying-down presupposes it.

They elevate earth, preeminently stone; and in truth the mountains are just elevated earth, stone raised into the heaven.

The elevation is decisive in that it inverts the usual order. As usually apprehended, the element of earth not only is beneath all things, underlying them, but even defines the very sense of underlying; indeed it is one of the two poles by which the sense of upward-downward directionality is defined for humans, living as they do upon the earth, standing upright from it while casting their vision upward toward the heaven, instituting a metaphorics that infuses and determines all others. In the mountains this element, usually underlying, becomes ascensional. Soaring skyward, the peaks reach into the region of the shining upper air that the ancients called *aithēr*. Their elevation into this upper region is visually confirmed as clouds take form around them or drift slowly across them. The inversion is, then, first of all, an alteration of region from one extreme to the other, from earth as underlying, as down below, to earth as reaching into the upper region. Inasmuch as the downward, underlying character is proper to earth, the inversion produced by the mountains sets the element of earth in a certain opposition to itself. Yet the inversion is also a reversal of the relation between earth and things. Though they lie on the earth or near its surface, all things come, with the inversion, to lie beneath the mountain peaks. To be sure, there are different degrees depending on the extent of the elevation. On the lower slopes where trees and other vegetation are still to be found, the degree is less: for the earthly element does not yet surpass things entirely but continues to underlie those things elevated to the same height. But the bare rocky peaks that soar above the tree line are more ascensional; towering above all things, they display the inversion more forcefully and are more enticing to vision. If, as here in the Dolomites, the peaks take the form of spiked, splintered shafts of stone, the inversion is even more forcefully exhibited, as the earthly element forsakes still more decisively its underlying, supportive character.

It is this inversion, indeed the force of this inversion, that can be apprehended in the spectacle of the mountains. And it is this force that gives force to the apprehension itself. It is not necessary to think about this reversal in order to be captivated by it; neither is it necessary that it be

Dolomites above Dobbiaco (Toblach)

recognized as such or conceptualized. The apprehension is energized by the spectacle; it is continually reanimated to such an extent that the vision exceeds apprehension, yet without becoming anything else. Before such a spectacle it is a matter neither of immediate apprehension nor of continuing observation but rather of lingering, of lingering before what continues to engage vision.

Relieved entirely of the supportive character otherwise definitive of earth, the towering peaks acquire a certain strangeness; they become remote from all the things belonging to the everyday, remote from all the cares of human life. They endure in their selfsameness; they remain aloof, removed, withdrawn from all the happenings in the human world below.

Nothing is more evocative of imagination than an element that both displays itself visibly and yet remains utterly remote, sheltering its secrets from vision, reserving them for the play of imagination.

With the arrival of a thunderstorm, all the elements came together, and all that is elemental in the mountains came to be accentuated and confirmed. As the thunder rolled on and echoed from one mountain to another, its spatial character was striking. Whatever may be the case with allegedly pure sounds in their confinement or with the sounds that signal happenings in the everyday, here in the mountains the supposition could never arise that sound is primarily temporal rather than spatial, that its sounding occurs across a temporal rather than a spatial interval. The time in which the thunder sounds is inseparable from the space in which it sounds. The sounding of the thunder—the sounding that *is* the thunder, for it is nothing other than the sounding—extends itself temporally only as it rolls on and echoes across the space of the mountains. The sounding follows the contours of the mountains, though without in any way reproducing that configuration. Precisely for this reason the sounding of the thunder and indeed the sight and sound of the storm as such were more powerful here in the Dolomites than in valleys to the north (such as Münstertal in the Black Forest) that are surrounded not by rocky, jagged peaks but by less vertical, tree-covered slopes.

As the storm was approaching, the rain could be seen in the distance. Long before it actually arrived, its approach was heralded by the cool, moist air, which reattuned nearly all the senses. The rain appeared like a veil over the mountain spectacle, at first more transparent, then becoming denser as it approached and finally encompassed everything.

22

Lumen Naturale

Near Umbertide
Umbria
30 July 2003

Driving across the Umbrian landscape at midday, our attention was drawn to the ever varying configurations of greens and browns, of forested patches and planted fields. The patchworks were especially visible on the lower mountain slopes, which effectively inclined the spectacles toward us. But on these landscapes what was even more evocative was the character of the light, bright and clear as in Sicily and Greece, yet softened and textured by this landscape.

Several hours later, near midnight, driving along an unpaved country road in a remote valley free of ambient light, we stopped to look at the sky. The night was moonless and perfectly clear. Ever more stars became visible, making an impression of uncountableness. Shapes and figures formed and dissolved and then formed again as our vision became more attuned to the darkness. It is easily understood how this very spectacle has always provoked elevation in thought and how, providing (along with the sun) the metaphorics of all metaphorics, it has lent its figure to the understanding of what humans are called upon to be.

And it will do so perhaps even more, if differently, as the spectacle is subtended by a theoretical vision that reveals an unendingness that the ancients, even with their still unparalleled cosmologies, could hardly have imagined, that we too can hardly yet imagine.

23

Mountain Time

Grossglockner
Osttirol
3 August 2003

We hiked up the valley on the southern side of the Grossglockner, walking as directly toward the summit as the contours of the valley would allow. We went as far as the Luckenhütte (a little over 2,200 meters). Farther up, the glacier was visible, though no doubt reduced a bit by this intensely hot summer. Along the way and again at the Luckenhütte it was as though the space of the mountain landscape opened another time, a time still governed by the elements, a time to which our own tempo had begun to accommodate itself from the moment we first caught sight of the summit. It is a time that prompts one to linger attentively in silent apprehension of the surroundings. It is a time that almost suspends time, a time of perdurance rather than flow, a time given rather than spent.

Thoughts returned then about the way vision is enticed by mountainside and mountain peak; but now I sensed more keenly the need to keep these visions intact and apart. Even if the words that would eventually come cannot but also broach what are called concepts, the conceptual is not primarily what counts when such thoughts are in play. Keeping them in play requires being guided by what is seen, though in a seeing, a sensing, irreducible to the mere registering of impressions. It requires resistance to concepts, resistance to the danger of merely reinscribing what is

View of the Grossglockner from the south

already determined in the concepts. It requires confronting language (and all its predeterminations) with the spectacle.

In the mountains certain inversions or oppositions are visibly broached. On the one hand, there is the ascensional character that is to be seen in the mountain's upward thrust and that is visibly confirmed by the contour of its peaks seen against the brilliant Alpine sky. Various features such as vertical ridges and striations contribute also to the ascensional orientation. On the other hand, there is the gigantic presence of the stone, its massiveness and its manifest heaviness. Nothing is more remarkable—as Gothic architecture attests—than the soaring of stone—of gigantic, massive, manifestly heavy stone—upward toward the heaven. In the mountains—as the mountains—such ascent comes about by nature, as elemental nature.

24

Of Stone

Dubrovnik
Croatia
5 June 2004

It is a city purely of stone. It is also an ancient city. Legends link the founding of Dubrovnik to the fall of the Roman city of Epidaurum, which in
turn had originated, it seems, as a Greek colony. For several centuries
Dubrovnik was ruled by Byzantium, and then from the fourteenth to the
seventeenth centuries it was a kind of Renaissance *polis,* like Venice and
Naples.

Yet today, largely as a result of the devastating earthquake of 1667, the
city's history is muted in its appearance. What predominates in its appearance is rather that it is a city of stone.

The old city is completely encircled by walls, in which are set various forts, bastions, and towers. The entire, unbroken circumference runs
nearly 2 kilometers. The wall itself varies in thickness from 1.5 meters to
6 meters (the thicker wall is on the land side); in some places its height
reaches 25 meters.

Not only is the wall as well as the various edifices set into it made
entirely of stone but also, most remarkably, it appears in many places as
though it had simply grown out of the natural stone on which it is erected.
Such an appearance is conveyed at every turn: a fortress, for instance, set
atop a mass of stone rising from the sea, looks as if it emerges from the

Dubrovnik, wall of the old city

Dubrovnik, center of the old city

stone. The blend of color and texture that defines the surface of the things crafted by human artifice is so similar to that of the natural stone that they are in perfect harmony. Even the marble with which many of the streets are paved seems not very remote from the natural setting of the city, a material taken indeed from nature but not removed very far from it. Throughout much of the city it is as though the stone were almost sufficient by itself to serve the needs of human dwelling and community, as though form were not of great consequence, as though it could just as well remain rudimentary. This formal simplicity is seen not only in the marble slabs and in the simple rectangular block construction of the buildings but also in the conspicuous repetition of form from one building to the next; along Placa, the main street, all the buildings are virtually identical. This appearance is not independent of the city's history, specifically of the impact of nature on that history: the earthquake of 1667 was so destructive that virtually everything had to be completely rebuilt, indeed—out of human need—as quickly as possible, hence uniformly. More recently, in 1991, the military-political assault that the Yugoslav (Serbian) army launched against Dubrovnik had a similarly destructive impact on parts of the city, though at this point genuine restoration rather than replacement seems largely to have prevailed. Yet, whatever the history, the appearance is now what it is: even where Gothic or Venetian Baroque elements are to be seen, they are muted, and the impression is, above all, that of the stone itself.

As we walked in the old city, we saw little that offered any contrast with the soft white of the stone, mainly just the red-tiled roofs and some green shutters. We noticed that some roof tiles were much brighter, much less weathered-looking than others, and we realized that these were the ones that had been replaced after the shelling of the city in 1991.

We walked throughout the city without seeing any trees or any natural greenery at all. The city is so devoid of vegetative life that we were quite surprised when we came across two or three small trees just inside its western entrance; they could not have looked more alien, as if they had been transported there from another, greener world into this world of stone. We had observed that outside the city walls it was quite different. Around the large hotels and the villas spreading up the mountainside, Mediterranean vegetation had been cultivated, including palm trees and orange and lemon groves. The contrast only served to bring out more forcefully the absence of vegetative nature from the city itself.

The island of Lokrum lies just offshore, almost directly in front of the city, protecting it from the sea. Though there is a good deal of greenery atop the island, only the slightest fantasy is required in order for it to appear as a huge stone floating in the sea, merely capped by a bit of green. Even as one looks away from the city toward the sea, the fancy of this floating island lets stone continue to dominate the appearance.

25
Protractive Places

Königstein im Taunus
Hessen
9 June 2004

There are times when certain places become protractive. These times cannot be determined in advance; there is no knowing when they may come, though certain conditions such as garrulity or abstraction may be recognized as inhibiting their arrival. Even less can they be brought about at will; at most a certain nonwilling expectancy, an awaiting, can prepare their arrival, yet without ever compelling it. They are quite unforeseeable, though their onset may instill a musical-like mood or even an enhanced sensitivity to music. Though such times are datable, what counts is not precise determination but rather those markings of time that link it to the course of things, that make it, for instance, a time of year, a season in which things of nature pass through a certain phase of their life. As when, in early spring, one sees—through a foreseeing animated by imagination—in the light green that has only begun to appear the entire course that nature will follow in the weeks to come, gathering in this time all that is to come, gathering to it even those times themselves that are still to come.

When such a time arrives, a quiet receptiveness comes over one's vision, opening it to the place to which it is thus attuned. Yet what is then released is not just a vision. It is not simply that one is enabled to see more clearly the things belonging to this place. It is not just that the contours of the things of this place become more distinct nor that their hues and textures are more finely discerned. Nor is it even just a matter of now seeing things previously unseen. While all these enhancements of vision may indeed take place, there is another alteration that is more decisive, a shift that is more transformative. When quiet receptiveness comes over one's vision, there sets in a certain drift of sense, and what one sees is set adrift between the two senses of sense. If other senses also come into play, they too operate within such a drift.

The two senses of sense delimit the most gigantic of intervals, that between the merely sensed and the most purely thought. The differentiation of these senses presupposes itself; it is therefore abysmal in the sense that no independent ground can be reached from which the differentiation could be simply carried out. For to distinguish sense as it is present to the senses from sense in the sense of meaning or signification is to put in play, in the differentiation, the second of these senses precisely as it is determined by the differentiation. In other words, to distinguish meaning as a signification of sense from the sensible or sensed as the other signification requires that one presuppose the sense of sense as meaning or signification and hence its differentiation from the other sense.

Yet when receptiveness to a place comes over one's vision, the difference will—as always—be already tacitly in play. What is distinctive in this receptiveness is that it releases a drift between these two senses. Then what is seen not only is present to sense but also exudes meaning. This occurrence is not a matter of conjunction; it is not an addition of sense to sense. Rather, what informs vision at such times drifts between the senses of sense. At such times there is a gathering of sense around the things belonging to the place to which one is receptive.

Then such a place becomes protractive: the place draws upon thinking, draws it forth, in such a way that thinking is drawn to such a place and enabled to draw from it. Words are evoked; they limit the drift, steady or impede the circulation, say determinately what has already been said in and through the gathering of sense around the things belonging to the place. The gathering of sense comes thus to be set into the form of determination, which writing then secures more enduringly. Yet in the operation that is released when a place becomes protractive, there is a double guarantee against mere closure: since, on the one side, sense exceeds word, a renewal of the gathering of sense is ever possible and, along with it, an undoing of the security of determination; and since, on the other side, word exceeds sense, it is ever possible for speech and writing to outdistance sense and to open beyond what will have been gathered in sense. Thus, while the expanse of topical sense protracts phonic determination and graphic enactment, neither sense nor word is capable of decisively closing off the other.

Between place and writer there is circulation. From the place as scene of gathering sense, there is a flow into the writing hand and, as inscription is enacted, a flow back to the place and the things belonging to it. The words drawn out by the sensible shining of these things in their topical setting are transported, in this sense, back to these things in such a way as to intensify their shining and to light up the place to which they belong. In the return of words to things, in the enhancing of their shining, in the illuminating inscription of place, there would be a double operation corresponding to the two senses of sense: things and place would be lit up as the sun lights up but also illuminated as an idea, concept, or signification illuminates. Or rather, the shining would be adrift between these extremes, so decisively indecisive as to undo the differentiation in the very operation that it nonetheless determines.

At such times in such places, there begins the movement that philosophy has taken and undertaken as an ascent governed by the value of light. Nothing has remained untouched by the force of this ascent and of the metaphorics of light that determines its course. Even when the course is reversed and at the risk of madness the metaphorics of light is inverted, everything remains as before. Merely reversing the values, merely standing everything on its head, changes, in the end, nothing. What must be learned is rather to join in the circulation, to give oneself over to the flow between the things of a place and their inscription. Then, persisting in receptiveness and reticence, one may begin to let the movement mutate into a hovering between the senses of sense, a hovering that would at once have begun to deconstruct this difference and thus, engaging imagination, would have begun to twist free of the differentiation that, almost from the beginning, has determined philosophy.

Writing, then, as topography.

26
Visible Elements

Fragsburg, Merano
Südtirol
14 July 2004

Snow seen on the mountain peaks at this time of year attests to an inversion in nature, as do the mountains themselves. It is not only that snow belongs to winter rather than summer, that it has been displaced from its proper season to one that is improper; but also that its persistence at the height of summer, under the blazing sun, lets a contest be staged between ice and fire. Walking in the mountains, we sensed this contest in the extremes to which our senses were exposed: the burning rays of sunlight and the cool, refreshing breeze. Here it was not just sight that was operative but other senses as well, most notably the feeling of sunlight or of cool air on the skin.

In the guise of mountains, earth thrusts upward into the region of air and sky. The clouds have an elemental and disclosive relation to the mountains. When they float across the peaks and their almost insubstantial mass expands, breaks up, and then again takes shape, the contrast serves to make the solidity and immobility of the mountains all the more manifest. Thus also it lets the ascendancy that earth here assumes appear all the more remarkable.

27

Cascata

Fragsburg, Merano
Südtirol
15 July 2004

Stone and water are opposites. One is hard, impenetrable, and immobile, the other pure fluidity, pure flow. Whatever is set in stone is secure and can endure the onslaught of the other elements; whatever is set upon water either sinks or else is set adrift at the mercy of the wind and the waves. Stone is, in every instance, determinate in size and shape, even if often, as in mountains, its shape is irregular and its size immense; water is the very dissolution of size and shape and can be given such only by containment.

Yet stone and water are not mere opposites in the sense of things or qualities that cancel each other. Their opposition is not of the order of what is called logical opposition; they are not contradictories nor even simply contraries. For they can—and indeed do—exist together; not, however, in such a way that their opposition is then canceled but rather in a way that preserves and even heightens their opposition. They come together in their opposition and thus engage in contention, in contest, doing battle, as it were, with one another, ever renewed battle.

As in an Alpine waterfall.

The path wound gently upward, the steep, wild mountain slope on one side, neat, well-tended orchards on the other. The fruit trees were not more than two meters high, and each was supported by a stake that ran almost the full height of the tree. They were laden with well-formed, though still immature, apples. The slope of the orchard made it possible to see how, beyond the rows of neatly planted fruit trees, the mountain plunged precipitously into the valley. Merano could be seen, too, as it spread out across the valley and up into the various passes leading beyond.

After a long, gentle ascent, the path suddenly turned steeply downward, and then, only a few steps farther, the magnificent waterfall came into view. There was evidence that at some time—perhaps before some subsidence blocked the passage—it had been possible to walk almost up to the waterfall; a rope bridge across the ravine remained intact, but there was no way to reach it, and there were signs warning one not to try. The nearest place from which to observe the waterfall was in fact the optimal location, allowing the entire spectacle to be seen in proper perspective. This place was directly across the ravine from the waterfall and at about the same level as the stone barricade behind which the fall ended, or rather disappeared as its impact was absorbed by the massive stone base. Looking upward from this location, we could see the opening in the rocks far above from which the long, thin cascade came plunging downward. Its fall was so swift and powerful that a great deal of effort and concentration was required in order to keep one's vision fixed either on a particular moving segment of the waterfall itself or on a stationary marker chosen in order to try to gauge the downward stream.

To be sure, it was sheer movement. Yet this long stream of water cascading downward was anything but homogeneous. Were moving water to become homogeneous, its very movement would become imperceptible, invisible. The waterfall, on the other hand, appeared in such a way as to display its headlong rush toward the stone base below. At the very top, where the water burst forth from a narrow crevice separating two fairly distinct mountain masses, it was churning so forcefully that no shapes could be discerned. But then, as the water plummeted downward, shapes began to form within the long, narrow ribbon. They shifted constantly; and yet, almost paradoxically, there was a kind of endurance,

Fragsburg waterfall

if not permanence. This endurance of the shapes is what, above all, allowed the waterfall to display its movement. Racing along the long band of water were certain discernible nodes, concentrations defined by a kind of whitewater effect. Though their shapes were ever shifting, they often took on an appearance suggestive of multi-pronged projectiles, each drawing along behind it an ill-defined comet's tail. As they neared the bottom, they disappeared as the stream was engulfed in the spray and disappeared behind the barricade of stone.

The two mountain masses that framed the waterfall seemed at first supremely indifferent to the incessant movement, the pure fluidity, housed between them. Yet the movement of the waterfall was so powerfully manifest that if, having focused for a while on the waterfall itself, we then shifted our view to one or the other of the mountain masses, it appeared—astonishingly—to move also, to the side, either toward or away from the waterfall, indeed in a direction almost perpendicular to that of the waterfall. The semblance of movement was so manifest that only the knowledge that these gigantic masses could not be moving prevented our being convinced. It was as if the movement of the waterfall was so powerful that it communicated with—dispensed itself to—the stone masses around it, setting them in motion, in a motion complementary to that of the waterfall.

At the bottom the waterfall disappeared behind the stone barricade, as if to conceal its own undoing, its degradation into mere flowing water. Farther down the ravine, away from the waterfall, in the direction of the valley, the water reappeared, though almost as if unrelated to that which only seconds before had come plunging downward. Flowing into the ravine from behind large stones and amidst the greenery nourished by it, the water made its way in gentle streams. Now the power was gone, and the water seemed merely to be carried along by the channels available to it. Gone, too, were the shifting, enduring shapes by which in the waterfall the powerful movement was displayed. Here there was only the gentle flow of water over stone. From this place on—as the streams coalesced and flowed on to the valley below—the contest had been decided, the battle won, water tamed by stone.

We recalled another waterfall seen in Austria a few days earlier: a single stream flowing down the vertical face of a mountain until at a certain point the outcroppings of stone split it into five separate streams, each of which then continued on its own to the bottom. Another strategy thus ruled the contest, stone articulating the very flow of the water, spreading it in its plunge to the valley floor.

Not even Hegel could remain unmoved before the sight of an Alpine waterfall. On the walking tour that he took in the Alps in July 1796, Hegel was remarkably unimpressed by most of what he saw, by the snow-covered peaks in the region of the Jungfrau as well as by the sight, close at hand, of a glacier. But it was different when he saw an Alpine waterfall, for unlike the static masses surrounding it, a waterfall presents the spectacle of sameness and difference in their coincidence. Hegel observed that one sees always the same figure and at the same time sees that it is never the same. Above all, what he found impressive was the powerful mobility displayed by the waterfall. At such a site—and perhaps only here—nature could outdo art: Hegel granted that not even the best paintings could capture the powerful mobility of the waterfall. For him this site offered a natural image of life itself.

It offers also a sight that exceeds every image: nature's elemental retreat.

28

Quiet Visibility

Near Lienz
Osttirol
6 August 2004

The clouds gathered slowly, as if held back by the high mountains on both sides of the valley. On the balcony of an old farmhouse, we could feel the change in the air, even though there was almost no wind; and the rain, when it finally came, fell lightly on the cornfield near the house and on the valley beyond. Clouds and mist veiled the mountains, as if to muffle all sounds. The quietness was something quite other than mere silence, mere lack of sound, not only because something could in fact be heard but also because it was a quietness also of what could be seen, a quietness that seemed prior to the very division between the senses.

Once the storm had passed and the clouds and mist had cleared away, the entire valley and the mountains on the other side were visible as before. And yet, something had been added to their visibility, an almost ineffable quality. In part, it consisted in the enhanced clarity of the air; but also it had to do with the way the jagged rocky peaks now appeared as they towered above the valley and above the lower, forested slopes of the mountains. It was as if a curtain had been drawn back, revealing them in their remoteness and aloofness, allowing them to show just how they persist in their utter selfsameness above and beyond the everyday cares that occupy humans. And yet, this very showing, its way of engaging our attention, attested that even amidst everyday concerns, we humans reach beyond, comport ourselves by nature to what is elemental in nature.

The independence and self-sufficiency of the peaks is displayed by their contour against the sky. Later, as dusk fell and the jagged yet continuous line inscribed by their contour was seen against the darkening sky, which obscures everything else, there was reason to doubt whether it is indeed true that there are no lines in nature.

In the mountains the natural order is inverted: what otherwise underlies and supports all things is elevated above all things. Though inversion is not violation and the result is not anything other than nature, humans are struck, captivated, enticed by the spectacle. Such would not be the case if the spectacle were presented to detached, neutral observers capable merely of recording the impressions received. Because we humans belong to nature and are always already oriented, in our very being, to the elements and to their belongingness to their proper regions, we are struck when this order is inverted. The disequilibrium that results, the impropriety involved in earth's ascent toward the heaven, is keenly sensed; and this sensing is, at once, a reattuning to the evocativeness of nature, a reattuning akin to the upsurge of wonder.

29
Shelterings

Boalsburg
Pennsylvania
15 August 2004

The way out and the way in are the same.

A door is the threshold both of the world outside and of the sheltered space within. It both opens upon the outside and closes off the inside. It both enables and prohibits passage between outside and inside.

As the inside is such that it can be opened to the outside, so the outside, the open meadow that extends beyond to the distant woods, is closed off by the boundary. Whenever it is a matter of topical spaces, of spaces that, at a certain place, serve for the spacing of things, openness and enclosure never function simply as opposites. Indeed in some cases they may be so intimately fused that the resulting space is best described as an *enclosed openness*. At least in such cases enclosure is precisely a way of holding a space open while also limiting its extent.

As in the shelters that humans build both as protection from the elements and from other alien forces and as the place where much of what belongs most intimately to human life comes to pass.

We had lived in the house for several years, and many of its spaces were haunted by memories of events, friends, insights, and undertakings belonging to those years. Both the size of the house and its construction were such as to emphasize openness. Its contemporary style maximized openness to the outside as well as between the various spaces within the house. The doors were made of heavy glass surrounded by a wooden frame; they provided security yet allowed vision to pass freely between inside and outside. Between the living areas there was free passage without any doors, indeed without walls, for the interior walls were largely cut away, so that this part of the house assumed the form of a single open space, of an enclosed openness. The openness to the outside was enhanced by the abundance of windows. Each window on the front offered a somewhat different view of the valley and mountains beyond. Those on the back looked out across a large deck to the woods, which came within a few feet of the house. Though it was a bit more exposed on the front, allowing some views into the distance even through the summer foliage, the back and the sides of the house were completely sheltered by the woods. Except for the midday sun, almost nothing penetrated this sheltered area between house and woods, its enclosed openness doubling that of the house itself. Yet here the patterns of sunlight and shade enjoyed a natural and free play that the windows of the house, however large and transparent, could never quite admit. This enclosed openness between house and woods also remained open to the sky, so that despite the enclosure the dimension of verticality remained in force, even beyond the canopy formed by the treetops. But what most of all distinguished this space from that within the house was the way in which the woods, while sheltering this otherwise domestic space, also sheltered itself. One could see the woods but could not see through the woods. Not that any absolute invisibility was in play: one could see into the woods, up to the point where the trees, bushes, and grasses blocked the view; one could enter the woods, extending the limit, though also then changing completely the perspective on the woods, seeing it from within rather than from without, still incompletely, still in such a way that much remained unseen. Whatever one's perspective, the woods prove capable of holding much in store, of harboring things so as to shelter them from the intrusion of human vision and control. Above all, the woods can shelter living things, animals, letting them, despite all intrusion, remain wild.

Doe at the edge of the woods, Boalsburg

    I was sitting on the deck, looking toward the woods, when suddenly a doe and two fawns appeared at the edge of the woods, only a few feet away. Their coming into such proximity is probably an index of the domestication they have undergone through frequent contact with humans. But this modicum of domestication hardly conceals at all the wildness of such creatures. Like all wild things, they slip in and out of presence: before their sudden appearance at the edge of the woods, I had not the slightest inkling that they would appear. They simply appeared from I know not where within the woods; and when a few minutes later they bounded away, I had not the slightest notion of where they might have gone. It was as though they were simply reabsorbed into the obscurity of the woods from which they had come.

The beauty of such creatures is attested by the way one's vision lingers with them, tracing and retracing their perfect proportions, admiring the fineness of their coloring. The fawns were only a few months old and still wore their spotted mantle. Not only the rich brown color of their coats but even more the delicacy of shape, equally apparent in the doe, brought immediately to mind the classical expression, though I remained absolutely silent, hardly uttering the word even to myself, for fear of startling them and dissolving the magic of the spectacle. What was perhaps most provocative was the look of the doe, not just her appearance but the look she displayed as she looked directly at me. It was a look that only a living creature can assume, one of utter attentiveness; her eyes were fixed upon me with a living stare that even the most capable painter could hardly have captured. To be sure, her look was not entirely devoid of familiarity, not entirely unlike the look of another person. And yet, in that look and behind it there was an unfathomable wildness, a wildness manifestly there in the look and not just cast back upon it from my knowledge that this was a wild creature. For several minutes we stared intensely at each other, simulating the visual communication of lovers, yet without the least bit of intimacy. Rather, her look was so uncanny that it ruled out any supposition of reciprocity. In the uncanniness of the look, the wildness of the creature was openly displayed, otherness that would forever remain closed off from human vision, an otherness uncontrolled and uncontrollable by human culture. Another person is always amenable to word or gesture; in receiving such signification, and even more in returning it, the other sheds the mantle of otherness. But the doe received nothing but my stare as it matched hers. Except for the merest suggestion of inquisitiveness that she showed by tilting her head now to one side and then to the other, she simply continued to stare at me with a look that yielded nothing.

There she remained until, sensing something, she became momentarily more attentive and then bounded off into the woods, followed closely by the fawns.

30

A Little Night Music

Boalsburg
Pennsylvania
22 August 2004

In Greece they sing most mellifluently when the summer sun is high over-head and the air is hot and dry. Whether from a clump of pines or an expanse of olive trees, their song sounds forth so ubiquitously that it is as if the trees themselves had become musical. Indeed it sounds forth with an intensity that matches that of the summer heat and with such uniform rhythm that we humans are easily lulled to sleep by their song. From my very first trip to Greece I remembered how tempting it could be: as we sensed with all our senses the heat and aridity that permeated everything, nothing could compare with a simple picnic there under an ancient olive tree, a few dolmades, some feta, some bread with tzatziki, a little retsina— then letting oneself be lulled to sleep by the music of the cicadas.

When, in the *Phaedrus,* Socrates tells a story about the cicadas, the set-ting is in the countryside outside the walls of Athens; while Socrates and Phaedrus are resting in the shade of a plane tree, the cicadas are singing overhead, as is their wont in such stifling heat. Socrates and Phaedrus resolve not to be lulled to sleep and indeed to continue talking in defense against the encroachment of drowsiness. By this means they will also avoid being laughed at by the cicadas and mistaken for slaves who, like sheep at a spring, have come to a resting place.

The story is that once upon a time, before the Muses were born, these creatures were human beings. But once the Muses were born and song appeared, some of the people were so struck with delight that they just continued singing and forgot to eat and drink until finally they died without even noticing it. Later the race of cicadas arose from these human beings. From the Muses they received the gift of needing no food but of singing from the time they were born until they died. After their death their duty is to report to the Muses concerning who on earth honors which one of the Muses.

This little story resonates with much of the discussion in the dialogue at large. A persistent theme in this discussion is the perfection of speech. One way in which speech can be perfected is by being cast as song. The story of the cicadas poses the measure of the power of song. This power is to be measured against the power of such basic desires as that for food and drink: the human ancestors of the cicadas were so captivated by their delight in singing that they forgot to eat and drink. The power of song is even to be measured against the power of death: when, forgetting to eat and drink, they finally died, they did so without even noticing it. Rather than suffering death as do less musical humans, they simply passed through it so as eventually to be reborn as purely musical creatures, the cicadas.

They are naturally musical. They make music by nature. Since they themselves are purely natural creatures, since they themselves occur by nature, their music is purely natural. It is music that arises purely from nature, without any artifice whatsoever. These natural musicians share their vocation with birds, also natural creatures who produce music by nature. Such music of nature appears quite remarkable if one considers how distant human music is from nature. Even the singing in which we humans engage requires that discipline and training be brought to bear on the natural gift presupposed in the singer. The music that we humans otherwise make by means of fabricated instruments is even more remote from everything natural. How marvelous it is, then, that nature itself makes music by assuming the guise of birds and cicadas! How intriguing, then, is the scene set under the plane tree, Socrates and Phaedrus speaking resolutely, giving voice to unnatural thoughts about the heavenly procession of the gods, while the cicadas, singing themselves to death, give voice to music that arises from the very bosom of nature!

Yet here in the more temperate climate of North America, the crickets and locusts—counterparts of the cicadas—do not sing when the sun stands high in the sky. Even in the season appointed for their song, there is nothing during the daylight hours to indicate their presence. Only with the coming of dusk do they begin to sing.

At first there was only a low hum without any rhythmic pattern. If I had not been just at the edge of the woods, indeed almost encircled, I would not have been able to hear it. From down in the village it most likely seemed that the night creatures just burst into song. After a while the hum subsided, and then, as if rehearsing, they would strike up a distinct rhythmic pattern for a few bars and then fade away. Gradually these segments became longer and the intervals between them shorter. Then I began also to hear other, distinguishable voices beginning their nocturnal song. Their polyphony was remarkable. I began deliberately listening for the different voices and trying to keep them distinct. But as the various voices sounded with rhythms that intersected and then disjoined in seemingly random yet orderly ways, I realized what demands hearing this polyphony made on my power of auditory concentration. There were different rhythms coming from different areas in the woods. From the left and the center came phrases consisting of four regularly sounded tones (of the same pitch), followed by a brief interval of silence, then repeated, and so on. From somewhere to the right came a similarly articulated phrase involving only three tones. From farther back in the woods I could hear a voice sounding three tones and then two tones (slightly different in pitch) with a brief interval between the triple and the duple. Once the concert began, there was a steady crescendo until their polyphonic song reached a fortissimo capable of drowning out human speech.

Nothing is to be seen of these nocturnal musicians of nature, but their presence is sounded in their night music.

The American naturalist Hal Borland called them fiddlers in the night (on fiddles given them of course by nature). He said that what we really hear in their music is summer passing. Like the cicadas in Socrates' story, they will sing themselves to death. By the end of September the woods will be quiet.

In such attentive listening to nature's polyphony there is a configuration that can be repeated in other guises. Suppose that in the configuration the attentive listener is replaced by a musician, a pianist, for instance. Suppose that this pianist is one whose entire existence is given over to music, one so engaged in his art that it emerges in everything he encounters. Suppose then that the polyphony to which he listens comes not from nature but from human conversations. The configuration would then assume the guise in which it is represented in one of the scenes in the cinematic production *Thirty-two Short Films about Glenn Gould.*

The scene is entitled "Truck Stop." As the scene opens, Gould is driving along the highway followed by a huge tractor-trailer. On his car radio a pop tune of the time called "Downtown" is playing. He pulls into the truck stop, parks, and walks into a typical truckers' restaurant; the same tune is playing on a radio in the restaurant. Gould takes a seat at a small table, and the waitress comes to take his order. Her greeting indicates that he is a regular customer: "Hello, Mr. Gould. Do you want the usual?" He answers in a gentle voice: "Yes, if you'll be so kind." These are the only words he utters in the entire scene.

He sits with his hands folded, looking quite concentrated; yet he tilts his head slightly to one side in a gesture of listening. To his right he hears a conversation—or rather, a monologue—by an older truck driver speaking to a couple others. The man is relating a story about how he picked up a hitchhiker whom he took to be a hippie, how the hitchhiker turned out to be a girl who had run away from home. The truck driver continues: "A hundred miles down the road I got her whole life story."

While the truck driver has been talking, Gould has turned his head to the right, obviously listening. Even as he turns his head back, he continues to tilt it toward the truck driver. Then, in the most significant gesture of the entire scene, Gould moves his index finger ever so slightly, then again and again, along with an even slighter movement of his middle finger. He moves his fingers exactly as he would if he were striking keys on a piano. This is precisely what he is doing, even though no piano is present.

He is composing what he hears, setting it into a composition that he is playing simultaneously on the piano.

As the first truck driver continues his story about the hitchhiker, the camera shifts to another driver who catches Gould's attention. He is sitting at the counter directly across from Gould's table. He is speaking French to the waitress, who sits next to him and pretends to take his order; obviously he has had something going with her. The camera now focuses on Gould's right ear; he has been taking in this conversation too, as, meanwhile, the first truck driver has continued his story, telling how finally he took the girl back to her home. Gould is listening simultaneously to both conversations and setting them into a composition, no doubt continuing—if only in his imagination—to strike the keys of the absent piano.

The camera then shifts from Gould's ear to a third conversation to which it thus becomes clear he has also begun to listen. The third conversation is between two drivers who appear to have been cheated in some betting enterprise. The polyphony is such that it is difficult to make out exactly what they say; in the midst of their conversation, the camera shifts to the counter, where the waitress is telling the Québécois that it's all over. As the camera turns again to the third conversation, the drivers are making a bet. Meanwhile the first driver can be heard finally bringing his story to an end; as the camera focuses head-on at him, he declares with great earnestness that he has never regretted the course of events that resulted from his picking up the hitchhiker, "not for a minute."

The polyphonic sonata comes abruptly to an end when the waitress brings Gould his unappetizing-looking plate. He picks up the ketchup bottle and opens it as the strains of "Downtown" are heard in the background.

31

Beyond the Narrows

St. John's
Newfoundland
8 October 2004

It is the oldest city in North America. In its beautifully restored ancient district near the harbor, the houses are painted in bright colors, which provide relief from the stony bleakness of much of the landscape of the island. It is also the easternmost city in North America, reaching far out into the Atlantic as if gesturing toward the places from which people once came to this new land. It is only a short distance down the coast to Cape Spear, the easternmost point of land in North America. If one stands at that point looking out over the sea toward the horizon, imagination will perhaps inevitably come into play, intimations at least of the uncommon vision that such sites can offer and evoke.

Yet, especially if one arrives by air, time may be needed to settle into such a place, to gear one's senses to what the region offers. I had been driven out to Cape Spear shortly after my arrival. As, driving back into the city, we came within sight of the narrow strait leading from the harbor to the open sea, my host pointed to the strait—the narrows, as it is called locally—and offered a casual remark that began to crystallize the scene for me. He was a person born and raised in this land, which seems to outsiders—though not to him—quite harsh and bleak; except for a period of study in Britain, he had spent his life in Newfoundland, and even the most

The Narrows, St. John's, Newfoundland

casual-seeming remark about this land drew upon his thoughtful experience of what life requires in a place where the elements are constantly at hand and hardly mediated at all. Pointing to the narrows, he remarked: "Beyond that, the next land you come to is Ireland."

In the days following, I repeatedly caught a glimpse of the harbor and the narrows. Then one day I set out to explore the entire harbor district on foot, knowing full well that it is in walking that one is best enabled to open one's senses to a place. The day was magnificent. Its intense sunniness was of a sort to be seen only in very northern maritime lands, as it requires that the sunlight be backed by an utterly cloudless sky and received by air that is very cool and crisp and entirely free of fog and haze. The sunlight glistened brilliantly on the water of the harbor, so brilliantly indeed that I could hardly see the water itself but only the patches of light on its surface. As I walked along the harbor, I noticed that the fall colors were just beginning to show on the long, sparsely wooded ridge that separated the harbor from the sea. I could only barely imagine how in a few weeks the severe winter would transform the entire scene.

The harbor has the shape of a long rectangle running parallel (north/south) to the coastline. On the seaward side it is separated from the coastline by a high ridge, which also runs due north/south. Toward the north end the ridge slants down to the water so that an opening is left between the end of the ridge and the hill that bounds the north side of the harbor; this opening is the narrows. On the inland side of the harbor, across from the ridge, the old town is situated; it was from this location, looking directly across the harbor, that I could best observe the narrows. Along both lengths of the harbor there were ships of various sorts and sizes, as well as shipping offices and various large pieces of equipment, a jumble of things that made the harbor lines look cluttered and congested. The south end of the harbor bespoke nothing but shipping and commerce: there were stacks of huge containers ready to be loaded onto ships and several cranes hovering over them as if in preparation.

Just as I was stationing myself at the optimal place from which to observe the harbor and especially the narrows, a ship on the other side of the harbor pulled out and headed for the narrows. It quickly passed through into the sea and was soon out of sight. As the ship glided thus from the enclosure of the harbor to the open expanse of the sea, likewise my vision traced the way from the congestion and industry of the harbor to the open, pure sea stretching beyond to the horizon. Or, more precisely, to Ireland.

The narrowness of the outlet had the effect of concentrating the vision, in contrast to the unbounded gaze out upon the open sea. Looking out through the narrows, what I saw was an almost linear—rather than planar—expanse. My line of vision extended beyond the narrows, beyond toward the Irish coast. The play of imagining, only intimated as I had stood at Cape Spear a few days earlier, now became almost spontaneous and, at the same time, remarkably open to reflection.

As I looked out through the narrows, my vision was extended across the open sea as if in expectation of seeing the Irish coast. And yet, the expectation was played out in a way quite different from the expectation operative in straightforward perception. In a sense there was no expectation in the form of an intention that my actual seeing might or might not fulfill, no expectation like that which is fulfilled when, turning to look at a previously unseen side of an otherwise uniformly monochromatic object, I discover that this side too is of the same color as the others. When, looking across the sea toward Ireland, I failed actually to see the Irish coast, there was no failure of fulfillment, neither surprise nor disappointment. On the contrary, when I cast my vision toward Ireland, I knew perfectly well that I would not actually see this land; I knew this not only in a theoretical sense but also in a way that belonged integrally to my very act of vision. I did not expect to see the coast of Ireland but only played at such expectation. I looked out across the sea *as if* by doing so I would see the coast of Ireland. In this play I might even enact imaginatively the voyage across the sea to Ireland by which I would be brought within sight of the coast of Ireland.

Yet I not only cast my vision out across the water, like a ship sailing through the narrows out onto the open sea. Also, in a complementary act, I drew back my vision, not because of the failure to see the coast of Ireland, but rather in such a way as to confirm the measure that casting my vision in this manner had supplied. What this double move of casting forth and drawing back provided was a measure of the distance to the Irish coast, an aesthetic measure having little to do with precise measurement.

Such imagining did not cease with the withdrawal or with the taking of measure to which it led. Rather, I lingered in the imagining, somewhat as one lingers in the contemplation of something beautiful; yet I continued, almost spontaneously, to librate between looking beyond as if to the coast of Ireland and drawing my vision back to the visible scene there across the harbor, just beyond the narrows.

In all of this play of imagining, there was no need to form an image, no need for a mental picture of the coast of Ireland. The imagining proceeded entirely without any images; it took place entirely within and around the visible spectacle, there beyond the narrows.

32

Force

Cataratas do Iguaçu
Paraná
13 November 2004

It can fall so lightly, so gently, that its exact identity is difficult to discern. Softly falling rain turns into dampening mist, which in the course of the night may settle gently on nature's surfaces and appear as morning dew or, in winter, as the delicate graphics of hoarfrost. Or in the guise of enshrouding fog it may lift as morning endures, deferring its return to the earth. But return it will, with inevitability, and, when conditions are right, with a force that demonstrates—if one can imagine it—the very forcefulness with which always, even in its lightest, gentlest disguise, this element is bound to the earth. Always, sooner or later, it falls to earth, but never more disclosively than at the site of massive waterfalls.

A major storm earlier in the week followed by two days of continuous, often heavy rain across much of Paraná had swelled the Iguaçu River to such an extent that, in the days following, its torrent supplied an enormous quantity of water to the falls. Once the rain had ended and the sky cleared, the visibility of everything was enhanced, and the contours even of the few scattered clouds that remained had that crystalline sharpness that only such conditions can produce at this time of year in the Southern Hemisphere. Better conditions under which to see Iguaçu Falls were unimaginable.

This most remarkable assemblage of falls lies on the border between Brazil and Argentina; the water coming over the falls forms the Paraná River, which then becomes the border between Brazil and Paraguay. In effect the falls span three countries and two major language groups; it is as though nature's excess at this site were such as could not be enclosed and contained by political and linguistic borders.

The Iguaçu River originates several hundred kilometers to the east near Curitiba and flows across the fertile farmland of Paraná, continuing as far as the falls. Even as the river approaches the falls, its surface remains quite smooth, completely lacking any signs of the adventure into which the water is about to enter. Indeed it would not be difficult to imagine oneself calmly sailing along or even just drifting along with the current, enjoying the heat of the almost tropical sun yet cooled by the river's gentle spray, only remotely sensing the force of the water, utterly oblivious to the impending disaster to which—were it not just imagined—one would be exposed. Only within a couple hundred meters of the falls do disturbances begin to appear. But even they are fairly slight, only a few rocks protruding above the surface with some small scrubs growing on them. The gentle rapids that result do not in any way portend the gigantic falls that lie just ahead. But then, just past the rapids, the earth itself suddenly falls away, and the water surges over the falls.

It is astonishing that there are so many individual falls. By the sheer force with which it is drawn downward when the earth falls away, the water has sought out every available cleft in the rocks and at each one, however narrow, has established a waterfall. It is said that altogether there are 275 falls, though it must be admitted that there are places where it is exceedingly difficult to determine where one fall ends and another begins. The difficulty in marking these vertical boundaries could serve as a reminder of a principle that was emphasized in Greek mathematical thought, namely, that only things sufficiently distinct to be marked as *ones* can be counted and hence numbered. Where boundaries can merge or where they are indeterminate, the very condition of counting and numbering breaks down. Here the use of number reaches a limit. At this limit, or rather, beyond it, arithmetic reckoning becomes largely impertinent.

Iguaçu Falls

What counts is the geometry of the site, taking this word to designate the figuration, the measuring out, of the earth at this site.

The entire configuration of falls extends along the newly forming river for about 2.5 kilometers. Its shape is roughly that of two arcs of 90° or more joined by a long linear segment. If one looks out at the falls from the path on the Brazilian side, then as one's eyes follow each arc in the same direction that one is taking on the path, each will be seen to curve around toward the Brazilian side; indeed the second arc, circling around toward the end of the path, actually ends up on the Brazilian side. Yet at the place where the trail begins, only the first arc is visible, and it was only as

I made my way along the trail that the falls along the linear segment and then those of the other arc came gradually into view.

The water that comes over these falls is not the clear, pure water of a mountain stream that has begun as glacial melt and in its descent has flowed only over sheer stone. Rather, in flowing across the fertile plane of Paraná, the water has picked up a large amount of soil, as if simulating, in advance, the falling away of earth and, in reverse, the water's inevitable fall to earth. Hence, in all but the smallest falls I could see clearly the earth that the water had brought along. As the water came over the falls, there were strands of earthy brown in the water, especially at the very top of the falls. Farther down, this brownish earth tone seemed to disappear, though closer observation revealed that in many cases it was merely hidden behind the spray thrown up from the bottom of the falls.

The path I followed on the Brazilian side was lined with lush semi-tropical vegetation. All manner of butterflies could be seen, and the extreme delicacy of these small wisps of patterned color made all the more conspicuous, by contrast, the enormous force with which the water came crashing down over the falls. At one point along the path I noticed a spider clinging to his web, which was some half-meter in diameter. While he pursued his course, awaiting his prey, my attention was drawn to the extremely fine web he had woven and, in particular, to the tiny droplets with which the spray from the falls had adorned the web, making it a bit more capable of catching rays of sunlight, even if also perhaps a bit less seductive for the spider's potential prey. As I continued, I came for a moment out from under the thick overhead vegetation, out onto a kind of observation point. For several minutes I stood watching the waterfalls, to which I was now a bit closer than back at the trailhead. Just as I turned from this wondrous sight and started back toward the main path, a lizard darted across in front of me. For a moment he stopped, and I marveled at how his body, covered with moisture from the spray, glistened under the intense sunlight.

Hundreds of meters from the falls I could feel the cool spray on my face and arms. As I came closer, the dampness became ever more pervasive, and, from a certain point on, everything along the way was thoroughly

Iguaçu Falls (upper and lower falls)

drenched by the spray. Indeed I could smell and almost taste the freshness and the moist coolness of the air. By this time the roar of the falls, heard constantly along the path, had become quite loud, and its intensity only served to concentrate my attention all the more exclusively on the utterly captivating sight of such enormous quantities of water pouring over the falls. Near such a sight all the senses are affected, and experience itself is intensified.

As everything became thoroughly wet with the spray from the falls, water began to drip even from the trees, the droplets sometimes falling along a shaft of sunlight, looking almost like a miniature cascade. It was as if even the trees were imitating the waterfalls, as if everything now was entirely shaped and determined by the phenomenon of the falls.

I noticed that many of the larger falls were divided into an upper and a lower falls, which were separated by a level expanse of water from which most often there protruded huge stones, some with bushes and even trees atop them. It was as if by such division each of these falls effectively doubled its force.

Finally, I came to the point where the second arc curves around to meet, at roughly a 90° angle, the endpoint of the path. Here it was possible to come within a few meters of a relatively large waterfall. In such proximity—perhaps only in such proximity—one can sense, with all the senses, the enormity of the force with which the raging water comes roaring over the falls and impacts the rocks below. Just a few meters downstream from the bottom of this falls, there were several large rocks protruding from the surface of the water, which swirled onto and around them. Atop the rocks were clumps of vegetation, their long, thin strands blown furiously by the falls, as if by a fierce tropical storm. Here, in the immediate vicinity of the waterfall, it was no longer merely a matter of something attesting to the force of the falls. Rather, it was a matter of sensing—in every sense and every sense of sense—this elemental force. To sense it with such intensity is also to sense that this force is such as to outdistance the scope of words; it is to experience the difference that sets the force sensed at such a site apart from all saying, that makes the force sensed exceed the force said in the word *force* and in every discourse elaborated around this word.

As I came close to the falls, its voice silenced all others. Its roar became so intense that I could hear almost nothing else, neither my own voice—had I not already been reduced to silence by the spectacle—nor the voices of others. It was as if the falls exercised a kind of suspension or reduction of everything else to insignificance or silence or both. Submitted to such reduction, all possibilities vanish before the actuality of sense, and—short of breaking the spell entirely—there remains no alternative but to give oneself over entirely to sensing with all the senses and in all senses such elemental force as was there displayed. To give oneself over to sense in

Iguaçu Falls (closeup)

this way requires force of imagination. It requires that imagination come, not to oppose something to sense, but to enable sense by drawing it into the most extreme engagement.

As I stood there before the waterfall, sensibly entranced by it, thoroughly drenched by its spray, I looked downward toward the area just in front of where the water came crashing down. There, created by airborne water droplets, was a miniature rainbow. I was reminded of a Platonic genealogy, the one endorsed in the conversation in which the young mathematician Theaetetus confesses his wonder, and Socrates declares that wonder is the beginning of philosophy. The genealogy is that of Iris, the rainbow, who was said to be the daughter of Thaumas and Electra; or—as the names, despite being proper, can be translated—of wonder and shining.

JOHN SALLIS is Frederick J. Adelmann Professor of Philosophy at Boston College. He has published many books with Indiana University Press, including most recently *On Translation* and *Force of Imagination*.